The Sovereignty of Man

By Dr. Chuck Missler

Koinonia House

The Sovereignty of Man
© Copyright 2018 Koinonia House Inc.
Published by Koinonia House
P.O. Box D
Coeur d'Alene, ID 83816-0347
www.khouse.org

Author: Dr. Chuck Missler
Editor: Amy Joy

ISBN: 978-1-57821-722-9

All Rights Reserved.
No portion of this book may be reproduced in any form whatsoever without the written permission of the Publisher.

All Scripture quotations are from the King James Version of the Holy Bible.

PRINTED IN THE UNITED STATES OF AMERICA

Table of Contents

Ch. 1:	The Question of God's Will	 1
Ch. 2:	The Case of Yitzhak Rabin	 7

The Jewish State 9
Hidden Codes and Rabin............ 13
Was Judas Guilty? 16

Ch. 3: Moses versus Abraham 19
The Waters of Meribah 19
The Mountains of Moriah 23

Ch. 4: Two Sets of Sovereignty 25
Ancient Meteorites................ 28
Moving the Sun Backward........... 31
The Triumphal Entry 32

Ch. 5: Hidden From Thine Eyes 43

Ch. 6: Ezekiel and Jeremiah............ 51

Ch. 7: Acts and Ruth 57
The Case of Paul 57
The Case of Ruth 61

Ch. 8: Calvinism vs Arminianism 67
Calvinism.......................... 67
Arminianism........................ 69

Ch. 9: Eternal Security................. 77
Security in Christ................. 78
Apostates 80
The Price of Salvation: 86
Things God Doesn't Know........... 87

Ch. 10: A Couple of Pitfalls............. 91
Pitfall 1: Works vs. Righteousness..... 91
Pitfall 2: Negligence 94
The Seven Letters.................. 95

- Ch. 11: The Prodigal Son............... 99
- Ch. 12: Triangles and Time............ 105
  - *A Little Relativity*................. *108*
- Ch. 13: The Door to Heaven........... 111
  - *Human Software* *112*
  - *Resurrection*..................... *114*
  - *Salvation* *115*
- Ch. 14: The Fruit We Bear............. 119
  - *Bearing Fruit*.................... *121*
  - *A Prayer*........................ *127*
- Endnotes........................... 129
- About the Author 133

Chapter 1

The Question of God's Will

Through faith we understand that the worlds were framed by the word of God, so that things which are seen were not made of things which do appear.

Hebrews 11:3

God formed man out of the dirt of the ground, and He created woman from the flesh of man's side.[1] We might not appreciate how personal that is. God merely speaks and worlds flash into being. God doesn't have to form things using physical hands that mold and shape. In His immense authority over all that is, He simply speaks and the universe comes into existence. Yet, the Lord took time to form human beings, fashioning us in His image and breathing into us the breath of life.

The Bible teaches us that God is all-powerful and there is nothing He can't do. His arm is not too short to save us. Psalm 147:4 tells us God knows the number of the stars, and He even calls them by name. Think of giants like VY Canis Majoris, a red supergiant with a radius 1400 times larger than the radius of our Sun. Think of the multitude of stars, the billions upon billions of them stretching deep into the universe. God can do anything He likes. Yet, when He made humankind in His image, He did something special with us. He created beings who, like God Himself, have the ability to think, imagine and create.

"Thy will be done," Jesus taught His disciples to pray.[2] How strange. Isn't God's will always done? We tend to think, "Of course it is. He's God!" Yet, there are verses in the Bible that suggest that the God of Eternity does not always get His way. That might seem a bizarre thought, but it's also true. We don't have to pray for the water cycle to take place or for the Earth to keep swirling around the Sun. Day and night, summer and winter will continue to the end of time, whether we like it or not.[3] Those are done deals. However, we know there are cases in which God wants something He doesn't get.

Consider this verse:

> *The Lord is not slack concerning his promise, as some men count slackness; but is longsuffering to us-ward, not willing that any should perish, but that all should come to repentance.*
>
> 2 Peter 3:9

Why does God have to be longsuffering? God shouldn't have to suffer at all, yet He waits with patience for those who will come to Him to be saved. Do all come to repentance? We know they don't. John 3:16 tells us Jesus died for the sins of the world, yet there will be human beings needlessly punished with Satan and his angels. Our sins were paid for, but some people do not repent of their sins.

Isn't that God's will? Isn't that what He wants? The answer is positively, No! He pleaded with Israel through Ezekiel long ago:

> *Have I any pleasure at all that the wicked should die? saith the Lord GOD: and not that he should return from his ways, and live?*
>
> Ezekiel 18:23

> *Say unto them, As I live, saith the Lord GOD, I have no pleasure in the death of the wicked; but that the wicked turn from his way and live: turn ye, turn ye from your evil ways; for why will ye die, O house of Israel?*
>
> Ezekiel 33:11

We all know about the sovereignty of God. God has the right and the power to do whatever He wants. However, we find a strange thing about God's creation; He has purposely made beings with the ability to make decisions that are contrary to His will. That's astonishing to think about, but the Bible clearly holds us responsible for whether or not we obey Him. When God made Adam and Eve in His image, He gave them sovereignty of their own.

We find a strange paradox in Scripture. On the one hand, we know that those of us that are in Jesus Christ were chosen and called by God. Yet, we also are told we have a choice to walk through His door or not:

> *According as he hath chosen us in him before the foundation of the world, that we should be holy and without blame before him in love: Having predestinated us unto the adoption of children by Jesus Christ to himself, according to the good pleasure of his will,*

Ephesians 1:4-5

> *I am the door: by me if any man enter in, he shall be saved, and shall go in and out, and find pasture.*

John 10:9

God has declared in detail the responsibilities He desires of His people, and the Bible lays out just how He is to be worshiped. I see books written about the sovereignty of God. I think the troublesome problem isn't the sovereignty of God. Even in our relatively naïve horizons, we can grant His authority and power. The real dilemma we wrestle with is the sovereignty of humankind. We find a basic paradox that seems to have gone on from the beginning - predestination versus free will.

The children have a riddle. Where does the gorilla sleep in the forest? The answer is: Anywhere he wants to. Like that gorilla, God can do whatever He desires. In His sovereignty He has chosen to give us autonomy, and He doesn't appear to take that from us. Our spirits are subject to us.[4]

How do we resolve this paradox? God has given us one of His greatest treasures, namely His Word. As jealous as He is of His name, He values His Word even above His name.[5]

> *The secret things belong unto the LORD our God: but those things which are revealed belong unto us and to our children for ever, that we may do all the words of this law.*
>
> Deuteronomy 29:29

In this little book, we're going to explore what the Bible says about this paradox. We're going to hunt down answers to the fundamental questions about salvation and our own particular part in the process.

Chapter 2
The Case of Yitzhak Rabin

Chapter 15 of Genesis contains an interesting hidden treasure that helps us begin to put things in perspective. That treasure concerns Yitzhak Rabin, but we need the context of the chapter first, as well as some history.

Genesis 15 is the chapter in which God first commits the land of Canaan to Abram, two chapters even before He gave Abram his new name of Abraham. God explains that Abram's descendants will be slaves in Egypt for 400 years, but He will bring them out and give them the land of Canaan:

> *But in the fourth generation they shall come hither again: for the iniquity of the Amorites is not yet full. And it came to pass, that, when the sun went down, and it was dark, behold a smoking furnace, and a burning lamp that passed between those pieces. In the same day the LORD made a covenant with Abram, saying, Unto thy seed have I given this land, from the river of Egypt unto the great river, the river Euphrates:*
>
> Genesis 15:16-18

Notice that the eastern border of the land is not the Jordan River, but the Euphrates. When people talk about the West Bank, they should ask, "of which river?"

Here in Genesis 15, God makes a unilateral covenant with Abraham, a commitment that is unconditional because it requires nothing from Abraham's side of the bargain. We learn two chapters later in Genesis 17:8 that God's covenant with Abraham is everlasting. This contract is confirmed consistently by the prophets, who repeatedly portray the future people of Israel as happily settled in the land after a time of exile. Even when the people of Judah were sent off to Babylon as a result of their sins, the land was still unconditionally promised to them until the end of time.

Of course, in A.D. 70, the Romans destroyed the Temple and Jerusalem as forewarned in Daniel 9:26, and before long Israel had lost its national identity. Israel became a trampled backwash part of the Middle East, ruled by the Romans and then by a variety of Islamic powers. During these years, Bible readers started to allegorize the promises made to Israel for the simple reason that the country had ceased to exist. They were wrong to do this, however, because even the desolation of the Holy Land was according to Scripture. Jesus warned His disciples about it in Luke 21:24, saying, *"And they shall fall by the edge of the sword, and shall be led away captive into all nations: and Jerusalem shall be trodden down of the Gentiles, until the times of the Gentiles be fulfilled."* That world "until" is extremely important.

The Jewish State

For nearly two millennia the Holy Land was passed back and forth between different hands, trampled and abused and neglected. Then, in 1948 the Jews once again came to possess the land of Israel. Since its 1948 Declaration of Independence, Israel has faced constant danger from its enemies on all sides, but Israel has also won every war thrown at it. Time and again, the surrounding nations have attempted to conquer the tiny country and have failed. From a backwash part of the Ottoman Empire, Israel has risen to become one of the most significant countries on earth. Well did Zechariah prophesy that Jerusalem would be a cup of trembling for the world:

> *Behold, I will make Jerusalem a cup of trembling unto all the people round about, when they shall be in the siege both against Judah and against Jerusalem. And in that day will I make Jerusalem a burdensome stone for all people: all that burden themselves with it shall be cut in pieces, though all the people of the earth be gathered together against it.*
>
> Zechariah 12:2-3

Here we see the sovereignty of God. Nearly 4000 years ago, God promised to give the land to the descendants of Abraham. God said long in advance that He would make Jerusalem a source of consternation for the whole world. We can anticipate that one day the people of Israel will have charge of all the land promised by God - all the way to the Euphrates. It may not happen until the Messiah rules, but we know God keeps His promises.

It doesn't even make sense that Jerusalem would be as important as it is. It has no harbor, no rivers. It's not on any trade routes. Israel has no natural resources of consequence. Why is Jerusalem significant? It's significant for religious reasons, because the Jews are interested in it. The Muslims let it go to rubble when they had charge of it, but now that the Jews want it, Jerusalem is suddenly the most important city in the world in terms of global stability in the name of seeking world peace. Zechariah's prophecy might not make sense, yet, in every major capital of the world, people are working overtime to develop their policies and positions on Jerusalem. As Nebuchadnezzar learned so painfully, God is sovereign over nations.

> ...and they shall make thee to eat grass as oxen, and they shall wet thee with the dew of Heaven, and seven times shall pass over thee, till thou know that the most High

ruleth in the kingdom of men, and giveth it to whomsoever he will.

Daniel 4:25

As I write these words, Israel has just celebrated its 69th anniversary. For nearly 70 years, God has protected Israel, and the Jewish state continues to grow stronger. Today Israel is at peace with Egypt and Jordan. Syria and Syrian forces in Lebanon are still at enmity with Israel and Hamas threatens from the Gaza Strip. Despite its rivals, Israel continues to be stable and prosperous. Israel has proved willing to remain peaceful with any country that is also willing to be at peace, but it has proved a great danger to any country that opposes it.

The "peace process" is no farther along now than it has ever been. The Palestine Liberation Organization (PLO) was founded on May 28, 1964 with the "liberation of Palestine" as its goal. Remember, Israel did not take control of the West Bank, Gaza, and East Jerusalem until the Six Day War in June of 1964. The PLO was not formed to take back the territories that Israel captured in the Six Day War but to destroy the State of Israel altogether. The decisions made by PLO leaders have consistently demonstrated a lack of interest in compromise or in true peace with Israel; this is because peace isn't the Palestinians' purpose. Their purpose is the ultimate extermination of Israel, but every effort to harm Israel has only turned its destruction on the heads of the PLO's own people.

In 2005, Israeli Prime Minister Ariel Sharon had Israel unilaterally withdraw from the Gaza Strip, removing thousands of Israeli settlers from their homes. This did nothing to bring stability to the region. In fact, Arabs saw the withdrawal as their own victory, and factions within Gaza immediately began bombing Israel. The result has been more than a decade of civil war within the Gaza Strip, four wars with Israel, and devastation to the people of Gaza. Sharon, long a lion in his fight for Israel's freedom and sovereignty over the Holy Land, was incapacitated by a stroke in January 2006, a few months after the withdrawal. He never recovered, and he finally passed away in 2014.

Israel's enemies care more about fighting Israel than about peaceful coexistence, and many people regard Sharon's stroke as God's own judgment for betraying Israel's right to the land.

Israel needs its extended borders for its own security. Cutting Israel away to its pre-1964 borders leaves it exposed and vulnerable to attack. No matter how any side feels about Israel, it's insane to leave Israel vulnerable and to thus destabilize the Middle East even more than it already is. It's possible that a nuclear confrontation will set the whole area on fire, and that's something nobody wants.

Zechariah promises that those who trouble themselves against Jerusalem are destined to be cut to pieces. That's a ridiculous prophecy for Zechariah to make, even in his own time. Why would the world bother itself over this remote relic of the past? Yet, we know today the central position that Israel holds in world politics and international relations.

All these things touch on Genesis 15 and God's ancient promise to Abraham. God is still sovereign over the nations of the world, and God can give the Holy Land to whomever He wishes. We see in Israel God's hand at work, even 4000 years after Abraham.

Beyond these things, we're going to see something *else* in Genesis 15 that really spotlights the central issue we're exploring in this book.

Hidden Codes and Rabin

On September 28, 1995, Israeli Prime Minister Yitzhak Rabin signed the Oslo II interim peace accords with Yasser Arafat and Bill Clinton. The interim accords continued a process of giving more governing power to the PLO as part of a plan to create a Palestinian state down the road. That all got interrupted on November 4, 1995, when a 25 year-old Israeli named Yigal Amir assassinated Yitzhak Rabin with two pistol shots. Amir confessed saying, "What do you want, for them to bury us in our own state? Rabin wants to give our country to the Arabs."[6]

This is where it gets interesting. In Genesis 15 God promises the land to Abraham. When we do an equidistant letter sequence (ELS) analysis of that passage, we find Yitzhak Rabin's assassination coded there.

For those unfamiliar with ELS codes,[7] the rabbis discovered that by skipping letters, they would find words and phrases hidden in the Hebrew Scriptures. They might count every third letter or every fifth letter and they would find hidden words. Today in the age of computers, we are able to search far more quickly and accurately than the tedious method of manually counting Hebrew letters. These ELS codes cannot be used to tell the future, but they do show God's fingerprints on the very words and letters of the Bible. For example, we can find eleven of the original twelve disciples' names coded into the text of Isaiah 53. We find Mary coded there three times, and James twice, because there were three Marys and two James, yet Judas is missing.[8]

So, what was written about Yitzhak Rabin's death? Coded into Genesis 15 we find in Hebrew: "Evil fire, fire into Rabin, God decreed."

It gets even more astonishing. The Jewish community has a reading program worldwide. From Rosh Hashanah to the end of the year, they read the Torah together, and most of the synagogues and devout Jews follow this reading program. Not only is Rabin's murder coded into the Bible, it is coded into the very passage in which God promises the Holy Land to Israel. What's more, November 4, 1995 was a Sabbath, and Genesis 15 was being read around the world when

Yitzhak Rabin was assassinated with two gunshots. That makes me catch my breath.

Yigal Amir, the assassin, took the position that he was fighting a war. He regarded Yitzhak Rabin as an enemy of the state, but the reality is that Amir shot down an unarmed man. While a majority of Israelis regarded Rabin as a traitor, his cold-blooded assassination still shocked the people of Israel. Except for a few extremists, the people did not condone murder and neither should we. Despite these things, we find here, thousands of years in advance, a hidden message that God decreed the assassination of an Israeli leader who was willing to create a Palestinian State in the land of ancient Israel.

Thus, we see the paradox of the Scriptures.

If God decreed that Rabin be killed, should Yigal Amir have been held responsible for shooting him? Wasn't the Prime Minister's death predestined? If God decreed it, apparently because of Rabin's rejection of God's promises to Abraham, then is the young man who shot Rabin guilty? Amir considered the assassination his own idea, done of his own initiative. Who is responsible for Rabin's death – Amir or God?

We encounter this puzzle again and again in the Scripture. From time to time we just slide over it, but at other times it hits us right between the eyes.

Was Judas Guilty?

God is sovereign over all things. James 1:13 tells us that God cannot be tempted by evil, nor does He tempt any man. Yet, we are told in 1 Peter 1:20 and Revelation 13:8 that God decreed from the beginning of the world that His Son would die for our sins. Jesus did not deserve to die. We deserved to die, yet God arranged from before Creation that Jesus would be sacrificed. This means that somebody had to do the brutal job of slaying Him, the very King of Glory. Are they guilty who put Jesus to death, when God had already foreordained it would be done?

What about Judas? In Psalm 41:9-10 we read:

Yea, mine own familiar friend, in whom I trusted, which did eat of my bread, hath lifted up his heel against me. But thou, O LORD, be merciful unto me, and raise me up, that I may requite them.

This verse is widely recognized as a prophecy of Jesus' betrayal by Judas. It was prophesied that Jesus would be betrayed and would be made a sacrifice for sins, but Jesus says in Luke 22:22, "*woe unto that man by whom he is betrayed.*" In John 13:27 Jesus tells Judas to go quickly to do what he had planned to do, but it was Judas who had purposed in his heart to betray his friend and Lord.

How do we handle this issue correctly?

Here's a question. Where is Judas today? He is in Hell. It's in the Scripture. Jesus calls him the "son of perdition" in John 17:12. Judas' betrayal was foretold, but Judas himself made the decision to give Satan a handhold in his life and to betray the Messiah.

We have libraries filled with discourses on the sovereignty of God the Creator. We don't really have a problem with God's power and control over the world. The thing that gives us trouble is a different one - it's the sovereignty of man. I haven't read any good books on the sovereignty of man, which is why I am addressing it here. God has given us an amazing gift in the form of our free will, but the level of responsibility is actually quite frightening.

Judas had a choice. He didn't have to betray Jesus Christ. We can speculate that if he didn't do it, somebody else would have. However, perhaps the prophecy would not have existed in the first place if Judas wasn't going to commit the betrayal. Either way, Judas had a choice, and he made it. His final decision was prophesied in advance, but Judas was held accountable.

Chapter 3
Moses versus Abraham

The Waters of Meribah

Moses gives us an interesting perspective in this discussion. In Numbers 20, we read about Moses and the waters of Meribah. The Israelites have gathered against Moses and Aaron because there was no water to drink. This is not a trivial problem. They have more than a million people and there is no water. Moses and Aaron fall on their faces before God over the matter, and the LORD tells Moses to go and speak to the rock so that water would come out for the people. This is slightly different than the previous time God had Moses bring water out of a rock. At Horeb in Exodus 17:6, God told Moses to strike the rock. This time, God tells Moses to simply speak:

> *And the LORD spake unto Moses, saying,*
> *Take the rod, and gather thou the assembly*
> *together, thou, and Aaron thy brother,*
> *and speak ye unto the rock before their*
> *eyes; and it shall give forth his water,*
> *and thou shalt bring forth to them water*
> *out of the rock: so thou shalt give the*
> *congregation and their beasts drink.*
> Numbers 20:7-8

This seems simple enough, but we see in the next few verses that Moses disobeys God's order. Moses is frustrated, and he has great crowds of people haggling him and wailing about what they don't have, still not trusting God after all this time. He is upset and not a little irritated, and he apparently doesn't think that words are good enough. Instead of speaking as God said, Moses strikes the rock two times with his rod. Water comes gushing out.

Moses has had forty years in Egypt and forty years herding sheep in Midian. He led the Israelites through the plagues and the Exodus. He's acted as their leader through the better part of forty years in the wilderness. He's tired. He's frustrated at the continuous complaining from the children of Israel. Instead of speaking to the rock, he whacks it a couple of times. It's understandable, but God has some words for Moses:

> *And the LORD spake unto Moses and Aaron, Because ye believed me not, to sanctify me in the eyes of the children of Israel, therefore ye shall not bring this congregation into the land which I have given them.*
>
> Numbers 20:12

We think this isn't such a big transgression. We can understand Moses' frustrations, and it seems like God is overreacting. Moses has been faithful to God with this massive responsibility on his shoulders. He's led these troublesome people for decades, and he makes one screw up and he's in the penalty box. Because of this incident, Moses is denied entry into the land of promise. He's allowed to see it from a mountaintop, but he's not allowed to go in. He dies before they go to possess the land, and Joshua takes over the leadership.

This seemingly small act of disobedience is quite a big deal for a lot of reasons. We can make an entire study of it. There is a whole list of subtleties involved here, and I won't go through them all because we have a different purpose here. However, a few things stand out.

First, Moses misrepresented God to the people of Israel. He gave the impression that God was upset, and God wasn't upset. That alone should give us pause. How many of us have been guilty of misrepresenting God? How many of us have failed to speak up when we should have, or have treated people roughly when God would have been gentle? The Third Commandment, *"Thou shalt not take the name of the LORD thy God in vain;"*[9] is all about representing God well. We've taken His name and we've stood under His banner. The challenge of our lives is to live by His Spirit, and by His Spirit to bear good fruits. The challenge is to reflect Him.

We also see in Numbers 20 that Moses took some credit for the water, saying in verse 10, *"Hear now, ye rebels; must we fetch you water out of this rock?"* Wait a minute. Who is fetching the water?

Moses and Aaron aren't. God is the One providing the water for the people.

I appreciate it when people offer encouragement to our ministry and let us know they've been blessed by it. However, there are times it makes me nervous. It's vital we remember that any fruit from this ministry is produced by the Spirit of God. We work hard, but it's God who does the real work that has lasting importance. We can do a lot of damage if we think we're the reason for any of it.

There's another dimension in Numbers 20 that can be overlooked, and I think it's the most important issue here. If Moses had done what God asked him to do, if he'd spoken to the rock rather than striking it, he would have offered us a model of the First and Second Coming of Jesus Christ. Christ is the Rock from which living water springs, as Paul tells us in 1 Corinthians 10:4. Jesus was only struck on His first appearance on earth. When He comes again, He will be the King. It's my personal presumption that had Moses done it the way God wanted to, it would become a type, a picture of Jesus. Moses blew the type, though, because he didn't do what God wanted him to do.

God did not foreordain Moses to blow the type. He didn't purpose Moses to disobey Him. God had a picture planned, and Moses smudged it. We are only able to see it because Moses had the humility to include the whole story when he wrote the book of Numbers.

The Mountains of Moriah

We find a contrasting example in Genesis 22. There, God asked Abraham to offer his son Isaac on a mountain in Moriah, and Abraham did exactly what God wanted him to do. God didn't let Abraham go through with the sacrifice of his child; God stopped him and provided a ram in Isaac's place. However, Abraham was ready to go through with the sacrifice of his precious son of promise, trusting that God was able to raise Isaac again from the dead.[10] Abraham was acting out prophecy, a father willing to sacrifice his son, and he knew it. He named the place Jehovah Jireh, "the LORD sees" saying, "In the Mount of the LORD it shall be seen."[11]

We know that 2000 years later Jesus Christ, God's only Son, was sacrificed - and I believe it was on the same spot. Genesis 22 clearly and intentionally models what God had prophetically in mind. Abraham was faithful to do exactly what God had asked of him. That's significant.

We see here two different instances in which God directed His servant to do something specific. In one case, the case of Abraham, the servant did precisely as he was directed, and in the other case, the case of Moses, he didn't. Because God's orders to Moses are recorded, we can see where they were going, but God had to make it clear that Moses' transgression was not a small one.

Did Moses go to Heaven? We know he did.[12] He didn't lose his salvation because he disobeyed God, but his disobedience did have earthly consequences for him.

Chapter 4
Two Sets of Sovereignty

As we study the Bible, we need to be more and more sensitive to the interplay between the two sets of sovereignty. There's the sovereignty of God, His power and His eternal plan, and then there's the sovereignty of man. God had a purpose in His orders in Numbers 20, but we see that Moses had a choice. It was not pre-ordained that he'd screw up.

This leads me to the little cliché about three things that God cannot do. I like to stand up before a group of conservative Christians and announce, "There are three things God cannot do!" I usually get gasps and looks of consternation when I do this, because it's obviously an obstreperous statement. I then go on to list the three things. First, we know that God cannot lie.[13] I'm not a heretic. It's true; God cannot lie.

Second, God can't learn. Why can't He learn? Because He knows everything already. That should be a source of comfort for us, because that means He cannot be disappointed in us. We can be shocked and disappointed by our own behavior, but God's not surprised. He already knows all things in advance, and that's why Jesus had to die.

There is a third thing that God cannot do. He cannot make us love Him. That's a contradiction in terms.

We think of love as an emotion, but it's actually a commitment. Real, solid *agape* love is an unconditional commitment. If I say, "I love you because you're beautiful," that's a conditional kind of love. What happens when you're not beautiful anymore? If I say, "I love you because you take good care of me." What happens when you don't take care of me? Human love tends to be conditional, but God's love doesn't depend on emotions. My wife wrote a book called *The Way of Agape* which gets into the differences between our human version of love and God's unconditional love.

God can treat us kindly. He can give us everything we need. He can protect us and lavish us with a home, family, good health, and a job we enjoy. None of that will make us love Him. In fact, it's often the case that living in comfort leaves us forgetting about God and not thinking about Him at all. When we love God, it is truly the response of our personal sovereignty. We have all stood at a crossroads where we have had to decide whether to obey God or to do things our own way. A multitude of thoughts and emotions and desires go through us when we reach these moments, but when we obey Him because we are committed to Him, that's loving Him. When we make a decision that we are going to trust God, that we are going to believe the best of Him at all times, no matter what our circumstances look like, that's loving Him. God can send us reassurances, but we have to decide whether or not we will trust Him. We are loving God when we believe He loves us just because He said He does.

God doesn't make us love Him, and therein lies the gigantic predicament of all time. As we go through the Bible, we discover virtually on every page a dance between His initiative and our response. We see His instructions to Moses, and we see Moses' response. Sometimes the Bible's characters respond properly, in His blessing. Sometimes they disobey and cause problems.

We see all through the Bible that man's sovereignty shows up. For instance, God had purposed to bring the descendants of Abraham, Isaac, and Jacob into the land of Canaan.[14] He had made that promise. However, one whole generation of Israelites died in the wilderness while they wandered for forty years because they didn't trust God to bring them into the Promised Land. We can make the case that the Israelites were not predestined to wander the desert for forty years. That punishment was the result of their unbelief. If they had trusted God, they could have entered the Promised Land right away, but God waited until the unbelieving generation died off so that their faith-filled children could take the land.[15] This is the interplay we see throughout the Bible, the jig of God's will with man's will.

Ancient Meteorites

Let me show you an example that I think is extremely interesting. In Joshua 10, we find the Battle of Bethhoron. Joshua has chased the Amorite kings of Jerusalem, Hebron, Jarmuth, Lachish, and Eglon to defeat them, and when they reach Bethhoron, some crazy events take place. We reach a famous passage in Joshua 10:12-13:

> *Then spake Joshua to the LORD in the day when the LORD delivered up the Amorites before the children of Israel, and he said in the sight of Israel, Sun, stand thou still upon Gibeon; and thou, Moon, in the valley of Ajalon. And the sun stood still, and the moon stayed, until the people had avenged themselves upon their enemies. Is not this written in the book of Jasher? So the sun stood still in the midst of Heaven, and hasted not to go down about a whole day.*

This is the famous long day of Joshua. Joshua was quite a warrior, and he wanted the day to last long enough for him to finish the job of demolishing the Amorites. God granted Joshua's request and lengthened the day. At first read we might say, "Hey. That's pretty neat" and not think much more about it.

While the typical Sunday School class might simply trust God's power to hold the world together - and rightly so - this is still a difficult passage for those who have studied astronomy and astrophysics. We normally assume that God had to slow or stop Earth's rotation on its axis in order to lengthen the day for Joshua. However, anybody with a background in astronomy knows there would have been worldwide catastrophe if the Earth had slowed its rotation on its axis.

However, there's a good potential answer to this. We know from the preceding verses that something massive was taking place in the Heavenlies. We read in Joshua 10:11:

> *And it came to pass, as they fled from before Israel, and were in the going down to Bethhoron, that the LORD cast down great stones from Heaven upon them unto Azekah, and they died: they were more which died with hailstones than they whom the children of Israel slew with the sword.*

We assume that these were regular hailstones of ice, but it might be they were actually meteorites. Stones from Heaven began raining down on the Amorites and smashing them. That must have been a terrifying experience, but the real miracle is that the stones hit the Amorites and not the Israelites. We see here evidence that something extraordinary was taking place in space, because what happens next is truly remarkable: the Sun stood still in the sky.

What happened that day astronomically? We know that the length of the year has changed during the past several thousand years. According to ancient calendars, Earth's orbit around the Sun originally took 360 days and it's suggested that Mars' orbit was 720 days. These were two planets in an orbital resonance. Because the orbits are elliptical and move forward a little each year (a gravity-caused phenomenon called a "precession") their orbital pattern looks much like the flowers on a daisy. Every now and then - every 108 years - Mars and Earth would have swung closely by one another, causing some noticeable astronomical events due to their forces of gravity upon one another. It's believed the most significant of these took place during the time of King Hezekiah, throwing off the resonance between Earth and Mars and forever changing the lengths of their years. For more detail on this, please see our studies *The Mysteries of the Planet Mars or Beyond Newton*.

If a near pass-by of Mars in the days of Joshua caused Earth's precession to change a little in its elliptical orbit around the Sun, this could have lengthened Joshua's day without affecting Earth's rotation on its axis.

What's fascinating about this passage isn't just its astronomical implications. It's that we have meteorites crashing down on Israel's enemies just in time to demolish them on behalf of Joshua and his armies. When did God put those meteorites into orbit? Certainly not the day before. Those meteorites may have been circulating in the solar system for thousands of years. What's more, they were placed just right to have 20/20 marksmanship and hit only the Israelites' enemies and not the Israelites themselves. I wish our ground support in some of our wars did that well.

Joshua prayed, and the entire Solar System was affected. That's astonishing. When we pray, we might be surprised to discover that God's responses to our prayers required preparation that took place long before we prayed. God knows the end from the beginning, and He saw our lives in advance. Does that violate our sovereignty? We can look at it two ways. We can suggest that God put into Joshua's heart to pray for that which God was already planning to do in the heavenlies. We can also consider the alternative: God prepared the answer ahead of time, because He saw from eternity past the thing that Joshua would request. Which is it? It might very well be a combination of the two.

Moving the Sun Backward

Since we're talking about strange astronomical phenomena, let's look at the major event that took place during the 8th century B.C., in the time of King Hezekiah of Judah. We find in 2 Kings 20 and Isaiah 38 this strange story. Hezekiah is lying on his deathbed, and he prays that God will spare his life. God grants his wish and says Hezekiah will live 15 more years. As a sign of Hezekiah's healing, God makes the sunlight on the sundial move back 10 degrees.

Because Hezekiah was allotted 15 more years of life, his son Manasseh was born, and during his 55-year-long reign, Manasseh did great evil in leading Israel into idolatry.[16] This particularly evil king would have not been born if Hezekiah had just died from that illness, however God still granted Hezekiah what he asked. God even offered to move the sun back on the sundial 10 degrees, altering the cosmos in the fulfillment of Hezekiah's request. The question, of course, is whether God changed the cosmos as a sign to Hezekiah, or whether the solar system was already in a transition stage, and God offered this sign because the Earth's orbit was getting shifted anyway.

God does operate in some pretty strange ways. He had the entire Roman Empire undertake a census in order to move two people from Nazareth to Bethlehem one Christmas Eve, if I can put it that way.

The Triumphal Entry

In Zechariah 9:9, we read an interesting prophecy:

> *Rejoice greatly, O daughter of Zion; shout, O daughter of Jerusalem: behold, thy King cometh unto thee: he is just, and having salvation; lowly, and riding upon an ass, and upon a colt the foal of an ass.*

The Triumphal Entry is Jesus Christ's famous fulfillment of this verse, and we find it described in all four Gospels.[17] The disciples go and get Jesus a donkey, and as He rides into Jerusalem, the people spread their clothes out before him, praising God loudly:

And they brought him to Jesus: and they cast their garments upon the colt, and they set Jesus thereon. And as he went, they spread their clothes in the way. And when he was come nigh, even now at the descent of the mount of Olives, the whole multitude of the disciples began to rejoice and praise God with a loud voice for all the mighty works that they had seen; Saying, Blessed be the King that cometh in the name of the Lord: peace in Heaven, and glory in the highest.

Luke 19:35-38

This was the time of Passover, when multitudes of Jews from all over the land converged on Jerusalem. It was mandatory for all able-bodied adult male Jews to attend three of the seven yearly feasts: Unleavened Bread, Shavuot (Pentecost), and the Feast of Booths.[18] They would camp all around the city, forming large crowds outside the city wall. This was the Passover season, and as Jesus made his way toward Jerusalem, the excited crowds flocked around Him. They'd heard about

Lazarus being raised from the dead, and they're celebrating Jesus.

In verse 38 they're singing, "Blessed be the King that cometh in the name of the Lord!" There are many times in Scripture that those of us who are Gentiles would miss something significant if it were not for the Pharisees. The teachers of the Law constantly come to our rescue by making a big deal about things that seem small to us. Here, the multitudes are praising Jesus, and we discover that they're singing from Psalm 118:26: *"Blessed be he that cometh in the name of the LORD."* The Pharisees hear this from the multitude of people, and they think Jesus should hush them.

> *And some of the Pharisees from among the multitude said unto him, Master, rebuke thy disciples.*
>
> Luke 19:39

Why do the Pharisees want Jesus to rebuke His followers? For celebrating His arrival? No, it's because they are declaring that He is the *Maschiach Nagid,* the Messiah. He is presenting himself as the King according to Zechariah 9:9.

The Pharisees presume that the people in the crowd are just getting carried away. They're thinking, "Surely, the rabbi doesn't want these people to blaspheme and call Him the Messiah." Jesus gives them a fantastic response that's not terribly tactful. He affirms the crowd's enthusiastic excitement:

And he answered and said unto them, I tell you that, if these should hold their peace, the stones would immediately cry out.

Luke 19:39

Psalm 118 is a messianic passage, and we should look at more of it in its context. This is a rich passage, and I encourage you to read it a couple of times.

I will praise thee: for thou hast heard me, and art become my salvation. The stone which the builders refused is become the head stone of the corner. This is the LORD'S doing; it is marvellous in our eyes. This is the day which the LORD hath made; we will rejoice and be glad in it. Save now, I beseech thee, O LORD: O LORD, I beseech thee, send now prosperity. Blessed be he that cometh in the name of the LORD: we have blessed you out of the house of the LORD. God is the LORD, which hath shewed us light: bind the sacrifice with cords, even unto the horns of the altar. Thou art my God, and I will praise thee: thou art my God, I will exalt thee. O give thanks unto the LORD; for he is good: for his mercy endureth for ever.

Psalm 118:21-29

We see a variety of valuable things in here. We know that Jesus is the "stone which the builders refused" because He quotes this verse in Matthew 21:42. Jesus recognized that He would be rejected, but that He would also become the head cornerstone.

The next verse is familiar to us as a Sunday School song: "This is the day that the LORD has made…" What day are we supposed to rejoice in? Certainly we can rejoice every day we're alive, but in its context this verse is speaking about the day the Messiah arrived, the day that Jesus rode into town on a donkey. That's a day to rejoice, the day the Messiah presented Himself. The LORD had foretold the very day that Jesus would do this through Gabriel's prophecy to Daniel, in Daniel 9:24-26. Our study *Daniel's 70 Weeks* goes into this remarkable prophecy in detail. The Pharisees should have known Jesus was the Messiah based on the 70 Week prophecy of Daniel 9.

God is sovereign. Jesus presented Himself as the King in fulfillment of prophecies that were centuries old. The people responded properly, but the Pharisees missed it.

Here's a question. Couldn't God have made the Pharisees understand and respond in accord? Maybe, but we find that they were free to embrace Him or to reject Him.

The day after His triumphal entry in Matthew 21, Jesus begins teaching in the Temple. He tells a parable about a vineyard owner whose tenants refuse to give him a portion of the vineyard fruits. The wicked tenants beat or kill every messenger he sends to them. Finally, the owner sends his own son, thinking they will respect him, but the wicked tenants conspire together to murder him. They drag the son out of the vineyard and slay him. Jesus tells this parable, then reminds the people that the rejected stone would become the corner stone.

It was purposed from the very beginning, from before Genesis 3 that Jesus would be sacrificed for the sins of the world. Yet, the men who conspired against Him had a choice. The vineyard owner wanted the tenants to respect his son, but they chose not to. Like the wicked tenants, the religious leaders of the Jews will be held accountable for their decision to reject the King of Glory. Jesus asks the people how the vineyard owner will deal with the treacherous tenants, and they have a good idea.

> *When the lord therefore of the vineyard cometh, what will he do unto those husbandmen? They say unto him, He will miserably destroy those wicked men, and will let out his vineyard unto other husbandmen, which shall render him the fruits in their seasons. Jesus saith unto them, Did ye never read in the scriptures, The stone which the builders rejected, the same is become the head of the corner: this is the Lord's doing, and it is marvellous in our eyes? Therefore say I unto you,*

> *The kingdom of God shall be taken from you, and given to a nation bringing forth the fruits thereof. And whosoever shall fall on this stone shall be broken: but on whomsoever it shall fall, it will grind him to powder.*
>
> Matthew 21:40-44

Within a few days, Jesus would be crucified, and He knew it. His sacrifice was always part of God's plan, and we see it all over. In Daniel 9:26, Gabriel prophesies, *"And after threescore and two weeks shall Messiah be cut off, but not for himself."* In Matthew 21, Jesus tells a parable in which the Son is slaughtered. Jesus refers to Himself as the stone which the builders rejected, quoting Psalm 118. Here in Psalm 118, we also find the order to "bind the sacrifice with cords."

Jesus presented Himself as the Messiah according to prophecy, only to turn around and present Himself as the Passover Lamb, also according to prophecy. Yet, the men who slaughtered Him did so of their own accord.

Remember the Israelites in the desert? They had watched God protect them while He sent 10 plagues on the Egyptians. They had been led away from Egypt following a pillar of cloud by day and a pillar of fire by night. They had watched God part the Red Sea for them. God had provided them water from a rock and manna faithfully every day. They had every reason in the world to trust God and put their faith completely in Him.

Yet, they didn't. They complained constantly. They constantly doubted God's power and willingness to provide for them and care for them. Ultimately, they refused to believe that God could give them the Promised Land. They were fearful and unbelieving, and so God made them wander for forty years until they all had died. He brought their children into the land, because their children were willing to trust Him.

God has His purposes, but we human beings were given sovereignty over our minds and thoughts and decisions.

So, we see Jesus stop to weep as He approaches Jerusalem during the Triumphal Entry. In a minute He will go in to cleanse the Temple, overturning tables and chasing people out. We think of His anger as He rebukes the money changers and salesmen. We don't realize that He has just come into the Temple after pausing to gaze on Jerusalem, grieving in His soul over their hard hearts and the destruction that lay before them:

> *And when he was come near, he beheld the city, and wept over it, Saying, If thou hadst known, even thou, at least in this thy day, the things which belong unto thy peace! but now they are hid from thine eyes. For the days shall come upon thee, that thine enemies shall cast a trench about thee, and compass thee round, and keep thee in on every side, And shall lay thee even with the ground, and thy children*

within thee; and they shall not leave in thee one stone upon another; because thou knewest not the time of thy visitation.

Luke 19:41-44

What else could God have done, except maybe put neon signs in the Heavens? He told them in advance. He had Gabriel lay out in their Scriptures the exact day that He'd present Himself, and they blew it. Jesus expected them to recognize the time of their visitation. He expected them to know Daniel 9:24-26 and to recognize Him when He came.

In Matthew 16, the Pharisees and Sadducees come to Jesus, asking Him to show them a sign from Heaven. In response, Jesus refers to certain rules of thumb for predicting the weather. We know these as a sailor's proverb, "Red sky in morning, sailor take warning. Red sky at night, sailor's delight." If the sky is red in the morning, bad weather is likely on the way. Jesus reproaches them because they can forecast the weather based on what the clouds are doing, but they are shortsighted prophetically. "*O ye hypocrites,*" Jesus says to them in Matthew 16:3, "*ye can discern the face of the sky; but can ye not discern the signs of the times?*"

In other words, they should have been able to recognize the times they were in. They should have been able to know that He was the Messiah according to the Scriptures.

Some of the Jews did recognize Him, but enough failed to embrace Jesus as Messiah that it spelled disaster for the entire city. Because they did not appreciate the true identity of Jesus Christ, some decades later the Jews sought to throw off the rule of Rome, just as they had thrown off the yoke of Greece during the time of the Maccabees. If they had recognized Christ, they wouldn't have rebelled against Rome. They would have realized that God had something else going on. In the end, it was a catastrophe. In A.D. 70 the 5th, 10th, 12th, and 15th Roman legions under Titus Vespasian besieged Jerusalem, murdered multitudes and burned the Temple. According to Josephus, 1,100,000 people were killed during the siege, and 97,000 more were forced into slavery.[19]

Palm Sunday should have been a joyous day. Jesus was riding into Jerusalem on a donkey as the King and He was on His way to conquer the sin problem once and for all. He was the Deliverer, and He had come just as the prophets foretold. Yet, He wept over Jerusalem, because He foresaw its future.

Jesus knew He was not coming to reign on David's Throne. Not yet. He knew He was coming to save the entire world, but He also knew it would be a long long time before His own people as a whole recognized Him, and He grieved over their destruction. He knew that full understanding was hidden from their eyes.

Which leads us to the other side of this puzzling coin.

Chapter 5
Hidden From Thine Eyes

Jesus says, "*but now they are hid from thine eyes,*" regarding the things that would bring Jerusalem peace.

Wait a minute. This suddenly sounds like God is responsible for Israel's blindness. Paul brings it up in Romans, agreeing that there is a period of time as a nation in which they are blinded. When the time of the Gentiles is over, the people of Israel will come to know their Messiah:

> *For I would not, brethren, that ye should be ignorant of this mystery, lest ye should be wise in your own conceits; that blindness in part is happened to Israel, until the fulness of the Gentiles be come in. And so all Israel shall be saved: as it is written, There shall come out of Sion the Deliverer, and shall turn away ungodliness from Jacob:*
>
> Romans 11:25-26

If God has given Israel partial blindness, then how is it their fault? He made them blind, right? Then why should He blame them for not seeing?

In Romans 9, Paul reminds his readers of Pharaoh, whose heart God hardened.

> *For he saith to Moses, I will have mercy on whom I will have mercy, and I will have compassion on whom I will have compassion. So then it is not of him that willeth, nor of him that runneth, but of God that sheweth mercy. For the scripture saith unto Pharaoh, Even for this same purpose have I raised thee up, that I might shew my power in thee, and that my name might be declared throughout all the earth. Therefore hath he mercy on whom he will have mercy, and whom he will he hardeneth. Thou wilt say then unto me, Why doth he yet find fault? For who hath resisted his will? Nay but, O man, who art thou that repliest against God? Shall the thing formed say to him that formed it, Why hast thou made me thus? Hath not the potter power over the clay, of the same lump to make one vessel unto honour, and another unto dishonour?*

Romans 9:15-21

There it is then. That sounds like we don't actually have any real personal will. God forms us out of clay, and we are whatever He molds us to be. Right? It sounds like Pharaoh had no choice. God hardened his heart so that He would have the opportunity to send the ten plagues and free the children of Israel from Egypt on the first Passover. Paul says it very plainly. God makes some lumps of clay into vessels for honor and others as vessels for dishonor.

Does that mean we have no part in the matter?

This is why it's so important to consider the entire counsel of God when trying to come to grips on these types of issues. It's easy to focus on Romans 9:15-21 and think, "Well, then it's not my fault that I'm selfish and rude. God made me that way." No, that's not what Paul means, and we need to balance this passage with other passages that deal with the problem of human sin.

Let's look a few chapters earlier in the very same letter. In Romans 1, Paul describes the downfall of those who turn away from God. This is interesting, because it gives us additional principles to work from:

Because that, when they knew God, they glorified him not as God, neither were thankful; but became vain in their imaginations, and their foolish heart was darkened. Professing themselves to be wise, they became fools,

Romans 1:21-22

First, we see those who knew God have their hearts darkened because they weren't devoted to God. They weren't thankful. They didn't glorify Him. They had the opportunity to delight in Him and be close to Him, but they didn't want it.

> *Wherefore God also gave them up to uncleanness through the lusts of their own hearts, to dishonour their own bodies between themselves: Who changed the truth of God into a lie, and worshipped and served the creature more than the Creator, who is blessed for ever. Amen.*
>
> Romans 1:24-25

They chose to turn away from God, and He gave them over to it. He allowed them to have what they wanted. They wanted to walk in their own lusts and to worship idols, so He abandoned them to the uncleanness they desired.

> *And even as they did not like to retain God in their knowledge, God gave them over to a reprobate mind, to do those things which are not convenient;*
>
> Romans 1:28

We see here a pattern. They did not want God, so He let them go. God is good and righteous and pure. God is love. They didn't want Him, which means they didn't want goodness and righteousness and purity. They didn't want love. They wanted to do whatever they wanted to do, and so He let them loose to be the carnally-minded people they wanted to be. Paul lists a multitude of things they turned to, things "which are not convenient," because they did not want to continue knowing God:

> *Being filled with all unrighteousness,*
> *fornication, wickedness, covetousness,*
> *maliciousness; full of envy, murder, debate,*
> *deceit, malignity; whisperers, Backbiters,*
> *haters of God, despiteful, proud, boasters,*
> *inventors of evil things, disobedient*
> *to parents, Without understanding,*
> *covenantbreakers, without natural*
> *affection, implacable, unmerciful:*
> *Who knowing the judgment of God,*
> *that they which commit such things are*
> *worthy of death, not only do the same,*
> *but have pleasure in them that do them.*
>
> Romans 1:29-32

These are people who enjoyed sin, and who chose their fleshly desires over God even though they knew they were doing wrong.

Lest we get the incorrect idea about where sin originates, James quickly comes to set some things straight:

> *Let no man say when he is tempted, I*
> *am tempted of God: for God cannot be*
> *tempted with evil, neither tempteth he*
> *any man: But every man is tempted, when*
> *he is drawn away of his own lust, and*
> *enticed. Then when lust hath conceived,*
> *it bringeth forth sin: and sin, when it is*
> *finished, bringeth forth death.*
>
> James 1:13-15

God is not taking people with no will of their own and making them evil. He did not take a Pharaoh who was tenderhearted and willing to love Him and then harden Him for the purpose of sending the ten plagues. No, God raised up *that* particular proud, stubborn young man as Pharaoh, and He made him ultimately a vessel for dishonor. He could have wooed the Pharaoh and spoken kindly to him and done everything He could to tenderize the Pharaoh's heart, but that wasn't the purpose He chose for this arrogant young ruler of Egypt. He didn't have mercy on Pharaoh.

What about Israel's blindness? Let's go back a minute to the parable of the wicked tenants in Matthew 21. Remember, the lord of the vineyard sent his servants repeatedly to collect the fruits of the vineyard. Finally, after they had killed and beaten and stoned his servants, he sent his son. The wicked tenants killed him too. So, what did Jesus say would be done to the tenants?

The people said, "*He will miserably destroy those wicked men, and will let out his vineyard unto other husbandmen, which shall render him the fruits in their seasons.*"

Jesus agreed. He tells them in Matthew 21:43, "*Therefore say I unto you, The kingdom of God shall be taken from you, and given to a nation bringing forth the fruits thereof.*" The chief priests and Pharisees knew He was talking about them.

In Romans 11, Paul says that Israel will be blind for a time. This was not the result of capriciousness on God's part, but a result of the constant turning from God among the Israelite leadership. They had rejected God's ways, preferring their own. They rejected God's Messiah, preferring to fight the Romans rather than humble themselves before God — and Jerusalem was destroyed as a result.

Even then, God is full of love for His people. In Romans 11:1, Paul declares that God did not wholly cast away Israel, for Paul himself was an Israelite from the tribe of Benjamin. As God had promised repeatedly in the prophets, He kept a righteous remnant among the Israelites.[20] Paul was part of that remnant, as were Peter and all the other apostles. God sent these beloved men and women out to be a light to the world, spreading the Gospel as was His original purpose for the children of Abraham.[21] Paul reminds us of the days of Elijah, when God had kept protected seven thousand men for Himself who had not bowed their knee to Baal.[22]

Chapter 6
Ezekiel and Jeremiah

Throughout the Bible, we see prophecy mixed with the will of humankind. We see God's purposes, and we see both human obedience and rebellion. Ezekiel gives us a glimpse of the sovereignty of God at work along with (or despite) the sovereignty of man.

In our own day, we have seen Israel become a country again. Every year, more children of Israel return from the distant parts of the earth to the land given perpetually to the descendants of Abraham, Isaac, and Jacob. The Prophets consistently tell us that God would do this — that He would gather the children of Israel from all the places they had been flung across the world. Consider what God promised through Ezekiel:

Therefore say, Thus saith the Lord GOD; I will even gather you from the people, and assemble you out of the countries where ye have been scattered, and I will give you the land of Israel...And I will give them one heart, and I will put a new spirit within you; and I will take the stony heart out of their flesh, and will give them an heart of flesh: That they may walk in my statutes,

> *and keep mine ordinances, and do them:*
> *and they shall be my people, and I will be*
> *their God.*
>
> Ezekiel 11:17,19-20

God says He will raise up the people of Israel and give them His Spirit and make them spiritually alive with tender hearts. This sentiment is repeated in Ezekiel 36, and then exemplified in chapter 37 in Ezekiel's vision of the valley of dry bones. God takes the dead, dry bones of the people of Israel, stands them up, puts flesh on them, and gives them His Spirit.

On one hand, a skeleton has no will, no power, no ability to give itself life. God's power is clearly at work to revitalize dry bones. On the other hand, there's human volition at work in the salvation of each individual. Remember, God implores the people to turn from their sins:

> *Say unto them, As I live, saith the Lord*
> *GOD, I have no pleasure in the death of*
> *the wicked; but that the wicked turn from*
> *his way and live: turn ye, turn ye from*
> *your evil ways; for why will ye die,*
> *O house of Israel?*
>
> Ezekiel 33:11

Peter understood this. Peter, who walked with Jesus Christ for three years and experienced the first powerful filling of the Holy Spirit on the day of Pentecost, Peter knew God's heart toward fallen humanity. He declared that God doesn't want anybody to perish:

> *The Lord is not slack concerning his promise, as some men count slackness; but is longsuffering to us-ward, not willing that any should perish, but that all should come to repentance.*
>
> 2 Peter 3:9

What's more, God judges each person individually, punishing those who rebel without partiality, and forgiving those who repent without partiality. Paul understood this just as well as Ezekiel:

> *And whatsoever ye do, do it heartily, as to the Lord, and not unto men; Knowing that of the Lord ye shall receive the reward of the inheritance: for ye serve the Lord Christ. But he that doeth wrong shall receive for the wrong which he hath done: and there is no respect of persons.*
>
> Colossians 3:25

> *The soul that sinneth, it shall die. The son shall not bear the iniquity of the father, neither shall the father bear the iniquity of the son: the righteousness of the righteous shall be upon him, and the wickedness of the wicked shall be upon him. But if the wicked will turn from all his sins that he*

*hath committed, and keep all my statutes,
and do that which is lawful and right, he
shall surely live, he shall not die.*

Ezekiel 18:20-21

Right now we see the people of Israel returning to the Holy Land. The land is open to them, and it's a fruitful place under the hands of the descendants of Israel. They are flourishing, despite enemies on all sides, since 1948. Yet, the nation as a whole has not acknowledged Jesus as Messiah. We know a day is coming when the people of Israel will understand who Jesus is, when understanding will blaze through their midst.

The two sides of the coin are seen clearly in Jeremiah as well, the part of God and the part of each person:

*For I will set mine eyes upon them for
good, and I will bring them again to this
land: and I will build them, and not
pull them down; and I will plant them,
and not pluck them up. And I will give
them an heart to know me, that I am the
LORD: and they shall be my people, and
I will be their God: for they shall return
unto me with their whole heart.*

Jeremiah 24:6-7

*Then shall ye call upon me, and ye shall
go and pray unto me, and I will hearken
unto you. And ye shall seek me, and find*

me, when ye shall search for me with all your heart.

Jeremiah 29:13

Let's be sensitive to this strange interplay between the sovereignty of God and the sovereignty of man. Man has the opportunity to screw up and he has the opportunity to screw up permanently. God will do incredible things to try to get man to avoid a destiny that is beyond our articulating, and yet God does not violate the sovereignty He has given us. They say that no one will be in Hell for their sins. They'll be in Hell for rejecting the provision God has made for their sins. That's heavy stuff.

Chapter 7

Acts and Ruth

As we study the Bible, we see the history of Israel as a demonstration of the sovereignty of God in His provision, woven like a fabric with the sovereignty of Israel in its freedom to obey God or reject Him, to ruin their lives or to seek His face. We can find a wide range of examples in this drama.

The Case of Paul

We remember from Acts 9 and 22 that Paul the Apostle was once Saul of Tarsus, who persecuted the Jews and had them beaten in the synagogues and thrown into prison.[23] While on his way to Damascus, Saul had a life changing interruption by Jesus Christ, and Paul became the apostle to the Gentiles. In Acts 10, the Lord taught Peter that He accepted the Gentiles as well, but it was Paul whose special mission was to go to the Gentiles.

Paul was a Jew and a Pharisee. He was taught by the great legal authority and Sanhedrin leader Gamaliel, and naturally Paul was passionate about the Law. As a Christian leader, Paul continued to embrace a deep love for his people, the children of Israel. And like Moses, Paul expressed willingness to trade his own salvation for the salvation of his people.[24] That's impressive. I don't know that I love anybody that much. No matter how neat I think you are, I'd be hard pressed to give up my salvation. Moses and Paul were stronger men.

In Acts 21, we find a very interesting situation in which Paul has a clear choice to make. He has traveled on all his missionary journeys, and he's making his way back to Israel. We find in this chapter two occasions in which the Holy Spirit warns Paul against going to Jerusalem. Luke tells us the story:

> *Now when we had discovered Cyprus, we left it on the left hand, and sailed into Syria, and landed at Tyre: for there the ship was to unlade her burden. And finding disciples, we tarried there seven days: who said to Paul through the Spirit, that he should not go up to Jerusalem.*
>
> Acts 21:3-4

Paul and Luke have made their way across the Mediterranean Sea. When they land on the coast of Lebanon, they find that the Holy Spirit has given Christians in the city of Tyre warnings for Paul against going to Jerusalem. Paul and Luke pray with these Christians and apparently take those words into consideration, but they continue heading south. They reach Caesarea on the coast of Israel, and they remain in the home of Philip the Evangelist. While they are there, they get another warning against continuing to Jerusalem:

> *And as we tarried there many days, there came down from Judaea a certain prophet, named Agabus. And when he was come unto us, he took Paul's girdle, and bound his own hands and feet, and said, Thus saith the Holy Ghost, So shall the Jews at Jerusalem bind the man that owneth this girdle, and shall deliver him into the hands of the Gentiles.*
>
> Acts 21:10-11

This passage is very interesting. The Holy Spirit has spoken through multiple people, warning Paul that danger lies ahead of him in Jerusalem. Paul's Christian friends clearly interpret the Holy Spirit's word for Paul as a message not to go. Paul understands the Holy Spirit's counsel in a different manner; he believes the Lord is preparing him for what lies ahead:

> *And when we heard these things, both we, and they of that place, besought him not to go up to Jerusalem. Then Paul answered, What mean ye to weep and to break mine heart? for I am ready not to be bound only, but also to die at Jerusalem for the name of the Lord Jesus. And when he would not be persuaded, we ceased, saying, The will of the Lord be done.*
>
> Acts 21:12-14

It's easy to get the impression that God actually doesn't want Paul to go to Jerusalem, and that might be the case. All the Christians, including Luke it seems, beg him not to continue on to his demise, and Paul is pricked to the heart over the situation. He's adamant about going, though, and his friends finally give up. Paul continues to Jerusalem, where mobs of angry Jews try to beat him to death, and he's handed over to the Roman authorities. From this point onward, Paul is in Roman custody.

Was it actually Paul's destiny to spend the last years of his life waiting for his trial and execution in Rome? Perhaps God had other plans for Paul, other things for him to do. We will never know, because Paul chose the path to arrest and imprisonment.

Whether God's first choice or not, the path Paul took still bore great fruit. Paul honored God, and he witnessed about Christ before the leaders of Israel and the world. We learn in Acts 24:24-27 that he spent two years often speaking about Christ with Felix the governor in Caesarea. After Festus took the place of Felix, Paul gave his testimony to both Festus and King Agrippa and his wife Bernice. Paul became a prophet to those aboard the ships taking him to Rome,[25] and during his years of imprisonment, he lived in his own house and ministered to all who came to him.[26] He made disciples of people within Caesar's household.[27] He taught an escaped slave named Onesimus,[28] and finally he testified before Caesar himself. A great many leaders of the Roman world heard the Gospel because Paul chose to go to Jerusalem and suffer in bonds.

Again we see interesting interplay between the sovereignty of man and of God. Paul had a choice. He had it in his heart to go to Jerusalem, and he went despite the Holy Spirit's warnings. His choice bore fruit, but it may or may not have been God's best plan. The Holy Spirit spoke, Paul decided to keep going, and God didn't stop him.

The Case of Ruth

I happen to love the Book of Ruth, especially as a book of prophecy. Revelation 5 only makes sense in light of the Book of Ruth. We know the story. Naomi was a Jewish woman who returned to her home in Bethlehem after sojourning many years in Moab. While in Moab, her sons married Moabite women and then both died along with her husband. Naomi would have therefore been destitute, except that her Moabite daughter-in-law Ruth had refused to leave her side. Ruth left her own people and gods and joined herself to Naomi, Naomi's people, and Naomi's God.[29]

Ruth is a rich book, full of prophetic types. We see here the story of a righteous woman who loves her mother-in-law and provides for her by going out every day and gleaning in the fields for food. We see here a love story, in which a wealthy landowner admires a selfless, hard-working Moabitess and falls in love with her. However, there's far more to Ruth than just a good story about how David's great grandfather met his great grandmother. It's a picture of Israel, the Church, and Jesus Christ the Kinsman Redeemer who rescues them both.

Naomi, the Jewish woman, represents Israel, and Ruth represents the Church, the bride of Christ. We see that Ruth meets Boaz through Naomi, and it is Naomi who explains to Ruth what to do to seek Boaz as her husband and redeemer. Naomi never meets Boaz herself until she is introduced to Boaz through Ruth. Boaz is the near kinsman who is able and pleased to redeem Naomi's lost land and marry Ruth. We see here the laws of Levirate Marriage and Redemption both fulfilled.

You might think, "Well, Chuck. That's all very interesting. How does Ruth apply to the question of predestination versus free will?" There are a couple of interesting things that I see.

When we understand that Boaz presents a picture of Christ, we can glean some valuable principles. First, Boaz sees Ruth and falls in love with her, and he speaks to his workers to make sure she's protected and provided for. However, he waits for Ruth to come to him. In the famous threshing room scene, Ruth does as Naomi has instructed her, and she lies down at the feet of Boaz, pulling his skirt over her. This is not a sexual proposition. In the ancient Middle East, the hem of the robe represented authority. When Ruth pulls the hem of Boaz's skirt over her, she is asking him to cover her with his authority. It's a proposal of marriage. Boaz understands this of course, and he's delighted. While Boaz treated Ruth with favor, and while he desired her, he waited for her to make the first move. As soon as Ruth makes her move, Boaz takes care of everything else.

We see another interesting thing in Ruth. A Moabitess, who was cursed under the Law[30] became the great grandmother of King David, and therefore the ancestor of Jesus Christ. A woman who was condemned by the Law was brought by grace into the literal family of God. This is fantastic, and it truly represents the position all of us face as Gentiles and sinners. We are all condemned by the Law, but we are forgiven and brought into God's family by His grace.

Did God intend to put that picture in the Bible? Did He predestine Ruth to that place of honor, or did Ruth behave honorably and lovingly toward her Jewish mother-in-law of her own accord? This is the very paradox we see throughout the entire Bible, and I suggest that the answer is *both*. God had a purpose for Ruth, and Ruth served Naomi, served Boaz, and served God faithfully of her own accord.

Boaz did not force Ruth to do his will. He waited for Ruth. We are not automatons. Jesus never chased after anybody and forced them to follow Him. He let them go if they chose to leave. We find the same message from Moses to

Revelation. He urges us to seek and knock on His door. He also stands at our door and knocks, but we have to let Him in:

> *But if from thence thou shalt seek the LORD thy God, thou shalt find him, if thou seek him with all thy heart and with all thy soul.*
>
> Deuteronomy 4:29

> *Ask, and it shall be given you; seek, and ye shall find; knock, and it shall be opened unto you:*
>
> Matthew 7:7

> *Behold, I stand at the door, and knock: if any man hear my voice, and open the door, I will come in to him, and will sup with him, and he with me.*
>
> Revelation 3:20

We are encouraged to seek God. Nobody can make us do this. It's something we have to decide to do. The First Commandment is to love God with all our hearts. We are perfectly capable of breaking all the other commandments. God does not force us to keep the First anymore than He forces us to keep any of them. Seeking and loving God - that's on us.

*Blessed are they that keep his testimonies,
and that seek him with the whole heart.*

Psalm 119:2

*And Jesus answered him, The first of all
the commandments is, Hear, O Israel;
The Lord our God is one Lord: And thou
shalt love the Lord thy God with all thy
heart, and with all thy soul, and with all
thy mind, and with all thy strength: this
is the first commandment. And the second
is like, namely this, Thou shalt love thy
neighbour as thyself. There is none other
commandment greater than these.*

Matthew 12:29-31

Chapter 8
Calvinism vs Arminianism

The classic puzzle between predestination and free will is well documented as the controversy between Calvinism and Arminianism. I want to take a minute and describe these two sets of belief that have so polarized the Christian community.

Calvinism

Calvinism is a set of beliefs that rose out of the teachings of John Calvin (1509-1564), the Protestant reformer in Switzerland. What we call Calvinism isn't precisely what John Calvin actually taught. It is a set of doctrines that Calvin's followers developed as a logical extension of his teachings. The "Reformed" churches are Calvinistic, as are many Presbyterians and Baptists.

Calvinistic teachings fall heavily on the side of God's sovereignty and predestination. They tend to reject man's sovereignty or freedom to choose God. These teachings are now summarized as the five points of Calvinism, and we often find them listed neatly under the acronym T.U.L.I.P.:

> <u>T</u>otal Depravity: Man is dead in his trespasses and sins, and because he is dead, he cannot choose God apart from God's work in his heart.

Unconditional Election: God chooses to save specific people, and they can do nothing to earn that salvation. From eternity past, God has destined certain people for Heaven and some for Hell, based on His sovereign will.

Limited Atonement: Jesus did not die for everybody in the world. He only died for those elected to go to Heaven.

Irresistible Grace: Those who are elected by God to go to Heaven are given the grace to know Him. God draws the elect to Himself and God's powerful grace cannot be rejected.

Perseverance of the Saints: The elected saints of God have eternal security and cannot lose their salvation. Once saved always saved. Those who walk away from God were never saved in the first place.

Now, there are different precisions of Calvinists. Some will agree that man is dead in his trespasses and sins, that God has to work in our hearts to draw us to Him, and that we can't lose our salvation. However, not all of these will insist that God predestines some people to Hell while they have no choice in the matter. Strict TULIP Calvinists, however, do go to the far end of the spectrum in their desire to honor God's sovereignty. These deny that we can choose

God at all unless He gives us the grace to do so. They claim that God must regenerate a person before they can even desire to come to Christ. If only those God has graced can receive Him, then the logical end is that God only graces those whom He has chosen to be saved, and the rest must be predestined for Hell. If only some are predestined to go to Heaven, then Jesus must have only died to save those people. That's the logic of many strict Calvinists.

Arminianism

The counter-view to Calvinism is generally associated with Jacobus, or James, Arminius (1560-1609). Arminius was a Dutch theologian who lived about half a century after John Calvin. He started out as a strict Calvinist himself, but then later modified his views. His followers expounded on these in 1610 in *The Five Articles of the Remonstrants*.

Arminianism is the theological basis for the Methodist, Wesleyan, Nazarene, Pentecostal, Freewill Baptist, Holiness, and many charismatic churches. Arminianism has a comparable five points to those laid out in Calvinism, but without a convenient acronym:

> Article 1 - <u>Conditional Election</u>: God is eternal, and He sees the end from the beginning. Those who are the "elect" are those God saw from eternity would respond to His Spirit and embrace the

Gospel message. The elect are those God foreknew.

Article 2 - <u>Unlimited Atonement</u>: Jesus died for the sins of the entire world. His blood is sufficient to cover the sins of every human being who has lived since the beginning of time.

Article 3 - <u>Deprivation</u>: Man is in a fallen state, and he cannot desire anything good in himself. He has a free will, but it is not strong enough to choose God without God's grace in His life.

Article 4 - <u>Prevenient Grace</u>: Without the grace of God, no human can want or think good things or withstand temptation. All the good we do or think is the result of our cooperating with God's grace and power working in us. However, God's will and Holy Spirit can be resisted. His grace can be ignored and pushed aside over and over until salvation is rejected forever.

Article 5 - <u>Assurance and Security</u>: A person who is saved by Christ is protected and assisted and cannot be plucked from God's hand by tricks of Satan. However, by his own will man can fall from grace and turn his back on salvation.

Those who follow the teachings of Jacobus Arminius believe that God's election is based on His foreknowledge. He knew long in advance what choices we would make and which of us would respond to His grace. Arminianists reject the view that God elects anybody for Hell. While Arminianists agree that we are unable to do anything good without the grace of God working in us, they believe that we can reject God's grace and the leading of the Holy Spirit. Some Arminianists do not believe that we are totally depraved and condemned as a result of Adam's sin but are only guilty when we choose to sin voluntarily.

There is a lot of debate back and forth between the Calvinists and the Arminianists, and the net is that both have good points, and both have incorrect ideas. Calvinism emphasizes that God is in control of everything, and that nothing can happen that He does not plan or direct, including man's salvation. Arminianism teaches that man has a free will, and that God can never interrupt or take that free will away.

Philip Schaff summarized the situation well:

Calvinism emphasizes divine sovereignty and free grace; Arminianism emphasizes human responsibility. The one restricts the saving grace to the elect; the other extends it to all men on the condition of faith. Both are right in what they assert; both are wrong in what they deny. If one important truth is pressed to the exclusion of another truth of equal importance, it becomes an error, and loses its hold upon the conscience. The Bible gives us a theology which is more human than Calvinism, and more divine than Arminianism, and more Christian than either of them.[31]

Both doctrinal positions are reasonable and have extensive Scriptural support for what they assert, and teachers on both sides embrace the Bible as the inerrant Word of God. I could have taken each of the five points and barraged you with proof texts for the five points in each camp. We can almost hear the echoes of the verses we've heard so often on these ideas. Yet, most of these points are partly correct and yet partly overextended.

The concept of total depravity, the concept that we're all sinners and inherit that genetic defect from Adam, is Scriptural.[32] However, the doctrine that Jesus died for the sins of the elect only is contrary to Biblical teaching. The Bible clearly teaches that Jesus died for all sins, and that everyone is able to be saved if they will repent and turn to Christ. Limited atonement is not a Biblical doctrine.

The Calvinist view can give people the misconception that God is capricious and quite cruel. While God has graciously provided the elect with salvation, He appears unnecessarily stingy in a way that is not remotely biblical. God as an abundantly generous provider. More manna fell daily on the ground than what the Israelites needed. We know this because Exodus 16:21 explains that the manna melted in the hot sun after they had gathered it in the morning. God is not stingy. He doesn't need to limit the blood of Christ. Jesus died for the sins of the whole world. Salvation is offered to all. Whether people rejoice and embrace that gift is another matter.

I love what Wilbur Smith says about that: "I'm glad He chose me back then because if He looked at me now, He might change His mind." Of course he's kidding, but nowhere in the Scripture does election get associated with damnation.

The Arminianist view can give people the misconception that we're all on our own. It can leave believers without a sense of their security as children of God. God certainly does have purposes and plans for us, things that He's created us to do. We are saved by grace and not our works, and yet God has prepared special jobs for each of us on this planet. We are all members of His orchestra, and He is the Director.

> *For we are his workmanship, created in Christ Jesus unto good works, which God hath before ordained that we should walk in them.*
>
> Ephesians 2:10

The Arminianist view can leave believers without a sense of God's purpose and destiny in their lives.

The best way to resolve the issue is to read the entire Bible, to survey all the verses that touch on the matter. We cannot do that in this small book, but it's clear that the Bible promotes both man's responsibility and God's power, grace, and constant work in the lives of those who serve Him. We see both working together:

Consider John 17, which appears to support the Calvinist view. Jesus is praying for His disciples, and He uses language that sounds like it would fit well with the points of Calvinism:

> *...Father, the hour is come; glorify thy Son, that thy Son also may glorify thee: As thou hast given him power over all flesh, that he should give eternal life to as many as thou hast given him.*
>
> John 17:1b-2

> *I pray for them: I pray not for the world, but for them which thou hast given me; for they are thine.*
>
> John 17:9

These verses certainly sound as though God has chosen those who are His, those who are saved. Yet even here in John 17 we find verses that indicate that people of the world are free to believe or not believe:

> *Neither pray I for these alone, but for them also which shall believe on me through their word;*
>
> John 17:20

> *That they all may be one; as thou, Father,
> art in me, and I in thee, that they also
> may be one in us: that the world may
> believe that thou hast sent me.*

John 17:21

The Calvinistic idea that God predestines certain people to Hell broadly contradicts other verses, starting with one of the most famous verses in the Bible:

> *For God so loved the world, that he gave
> his only begotten Son, that whosoever
> believeth in him should not perish, but
> have everlasting life.*

John 3:16

What does it say? God so loved the "world" - not just the "elect." What else does it say? It says, "*that whosoever believeth.*" It doesn't say "those whom God chose" but "*whosoever.*" We find balancing verses throughout the Bible, verses that contribute to the entire picture. In the introduction of his Gospel, John offers a verse that provides us with both sides of the coin - those who believe, and God who gives life:

> *But as many as received him, to them gave
> he power to become the sons of God,
> even to them that believe on his name:
> Which were born, not of blood, nor of the
> will of the flesh, nor of the will of man,
> but of God.*

John 1:12-13

In its extreme form, Calvinism denies man's responsibility to seek God with all his heart. In its extreme form, Arminianism leads to the belief that if a believer sins, he has lost his salvation and he must be born again and again and again. The truth is a river that flows between these two extremes.

Of course, if we can accept God and reject Him of our own accord, can we lose our salvation? All of us have feared at times that we've gone beyond God's forgiveness and might be doomed to Hell, but is that scriptural?

Chapter 9
Eternal Security

Can we lose our salvation? This is a heavy question. More than seven decades ago, I believed that Jesus paid for my sins, but there have certainly been times I've sinned in the thousands upon thousands of days since. There have been times when I didn't listen to God as I should, when I was far more focused on what I wanted to do than what God wanted to do in me. Was I in danger of losing my salvation during those years? That's a terrifying idea.

This is a big issue, because some Christians fear from day to day about whether they are saved. These dear souls beg God's forgiveness at the altar every time they go to church because they are in constant fear of losing their salvation. On the other hand, others have no fear of God at all, wantonly doing whatever they like because they gave their lives to Christ once years before and assume they're on their way to heaven. It's important to have a Biblical view in this debate.

The Calvinist doctrine teaches that we who are saved were predestined before the foundation of the world. It was God who chose us, and we are saved only by the initiative of and the completed work of Jesus Christ. God made us alive in Christ in the first place, giving us the ability to know Him and serve Him, so it is impossible for us to destroy the work that God has done. We have been born again, and there is no way to become unborn. Since we did not earn our salvation in any way - it is a completely free gift - then there is no way we can lose it.

Arminianists disagree. Their doctrine teaches that God gave us free will. They believe that we cannot choose God without His grace working within us, but we decide whether to embrace that grace and to walk with Christ. Because we are saved only as long as we abide in Christ, we also have the possibility of falling away.

We can ask which one is correct, but that's not the real question. They are both correct, but they are both incomplete.

Security in Christ

There is clear Scripture to give us confidence that those who are truly born again, who have trusted the Lord Jesus Christ for salvation are secure. When we accept Jesus Christ as our Savior, we are born again. We have been adopted into God's family as His children:[33] We are new creations in Christ.

> *Therefore if any man be in Christ, he is a new creature: old things are passed away; behold, all things are become new.*
> 2 Corinthians 5:17

It's the Shepherd's job to keep the sheep; they don't keep themselves. We may stumble, we may backslide, we may lose rewards, but we are sealed by the Holy Spirit, and Jesus is able to keep us in Him until the Judgment Day.

> *My sheep hear my voice, and I know them, and they follow me: And I give unto them eternal life; and they shall never perish, neither shall any man pluck them out of my hand. My Father, which gave them me, is greater than all; and no man is able to pluck them out of my Father's hand.*
>
> John 10:27-29

> *For I am persuaded, that neither death, nor life, nor angels, nor principalities, nor powers, nor things present, nor things to come, Nor height, nor depth, nor any other creature, shall be able to separate us from the love of God, which is in Christ Jesus our Lord.*
>
> Romans 8:38-39

> *In whom ye also trusted, after that ye heard the word of truth, the gospel of your salvation: in whom also after that ye believed, ye were sealed with that holy Spirit of promise, Which is the earnest of our inheritance until the redemption of the purchased possession, unto the praise of his glory.*
>
> Ephesians 1:13-14

> *Now unto him that is able to keep you from falling, and to present you faultless before the presence of his glory with exceeding joy, To the only wise God our Saviour, be glory and majesty, dominion and power, both now and ever. Amen.*
>
> Jude 1:24-25

The Bible says these things clearly. When Jesus says nobody is able to pluck His sheep from His hand, we trust that means us too.

Apostates

However, that doesn't mean there isn't opportunity for apostasy - for walking away from the Lord. Judas followed Jesus for three years, but then he turned around and betrayed him. Jesus calls him the "son of perdition," and it's easy to make the case that Judas was never saved in the first place. He was always going to be the man who betrayed Jesus, and Jesus knew it from the beginning.

Jesus told a parable of ten virgins in Matthew 25:1-13. Five were wise and brought extra oil, and five were foolish and did not. We all need to be ready and waiting for Christ. As long as we are ready and waiting, we don't have to fear that we'll miss Him.

We find plenty of warnings against false teachers and false prophets in the New Testament. We meet people in our lives who know how to say all the right things, but their hearts are actually far from God. We can all think of certain preachers and televangelists who have gotten rich on the Gospel; Peter warns us against these people.

> *But there were false prophets also among the people, even as there shall be false teachers among you, who privily shall bring in damnable heresies, even denying the Lord that bought them, and bring upon themselves swift destruction. And many shall follow their pernicious ways; by reason of whom the way of truth shall be evil spoken of. And through covetousness shall they with feigned words make merchandise of you: whose judgment now of a long time lingereth not, and their damnation slumbereth not.*
>
> 2 Peter 2:1-3

We also find mention of people — church-going people — who apparently don't really understand the Spirit and heart of God. They look good on the outside, but they don't receive the truth in their hearts. Paul warns Timothy about those kinds of Christians, who say they serve God but actually do not follow Him after all:

> *For the time will come when they will not endure sound doctrine; but after their own lusts shall they heap to themselves teachers, having itching ears; And they shall turn*

*away their ears from the truth, and shall
be turned unto fables.*

2 Timothy 4:3-4

We are able to find plenty of churches like this today. The people in them go to weekly services, but they attend sermons where they hear what they want to hear. They are not hungry for the actual truth of God, and their lives look nothing like Jesus Christ when they leave the church doors.

However, Jesus also tells us about another group of people, the short-lived believers. There are some people who hear the Word and are excited about the Gospel, but their faith dies because their roots never get deep. The seed of the Word grows for a time, but then the young plant dies. Remember Christ's parable of the scattered seed in Matthew 13, Mark 4, and Luke 8? The seed fell on the hard road, on the rocks, among the thorns, and into good soil. Only in good soil did the seed grow to bear fruit.

> *They on the rock are they, which, when they hear, receive the word with joy; and these have no root, which for a while believe, and in time of temptation fall away. And that which fell among thorns are they, which, when they have heard, go forth, and are choked with cares and riches and pleasures of this life, and bring no fruit to perfection.*

Luke 8:13-14

Does that mean there's no hope for the rocky soil or the thorny soil? No, we can pray for the stony and thorny hearts. We can pray for ourselves, "Lord, please show me what it takes to get these rocks out of my heart." The rocky, thorny soil can be cleared. However, there's a place to say that some people can hear the Gospel with joy, but then they turn away and forget about it and go on with their lives. Were they ever truly saved? Not from the perspective of eternity. God knows who are His, because He sees things from outside of time.

It comes down to the difference between true faith, true inner heart belief, and a temporary good idea. We can walk down the sawdust trail at a Billy Graham crusade, and that might be the moment of true faith and trust in Christ, or it might be the moment where we expressed what we thought was a good idea at the time. One leads to salvation, and the other does not.

The thief on the cross in Luke 23 believed in Jesus, and that's all it took. Jesus told him they would see each other in Paradise.[34] That thief expressed true faith. Hanging on the cross in his last moments after a life of sin, his sins were forgiven. Not by works of righteousness which we have done, but according to His mercy, He has saved us.[35] Yet, how many people who want salvation actually want to follow Jesus Christ?

There are places in the Bible that describe people who have served God but then end up falling away. Consider Demas, Paul's fellow servant in the Gospel. We hear about him in a couple of epistles before we learn that he's gone back into the world. In Colossians 4:14, Paul sends the greetings of Luke "the beloved physicians" along with the greetings of Demas. In Philemon, we also find Demas listed as Paul's fellow laborer. At the end of his life, however, Paul tells Timothy that Demas has abandoned him.

For Demas hath forsaken me, having loved this present world, and is departed unto Thessalonica; Crescens to Galatia, Titus unto Dalmatia.

2 Timothy 4:10

This is a tragic sort of verse. Paul tells Timothy that everybody has left him. It says nothing of Demas' salvation. Demas might have had business to attend to that Paul just didn't understand. We don't know the struggle of Demas here. Still, it's a sobering verse. Did Demas lose his salvation, or did Demas just disappoint his friend?

Then, we have this terrifying passage in Hebrews, a passage that gives us all a sense of dread:

For it is impossible for those who were once enlightened, and have tasted of the Heavenly gift, and were made partakers of the Holy Ghost, And have tasted the good word of God, and the powers of the world to come, If they shall fall away, to renew them again unto repentance; seeing they crucify to themselves the Son of God afresh, and put him to an open shame.

Hebrews 6:4-6

This is probably one of the most frightening passages in all the Bible. The writer of Hebrews makes us all think of those things we've done: those sins we've committed, those times we told God, "I'm doing it my way for awhile." Have we crucified the Son of God afresh and put Him to open shame again? Are we guilty of that, and can we ever be forgiven?

When we are fearful in this way, we have to remember Peter. Thank you, Father, for Peter. Peter had followed Jesus for three years. He'd seen Jesus do great works day after day. He knew the power of his Lord, and he had vowed to go to death for Christ. Yet, that very night Peter was questioned by a little servant girl, and he denied Jesus three times.[36] Peter the big fisherman, the leader of the disciples, Peter denied Jesus.

Did Jesus throw Peter away? No, of course not. Did Jesus love Peter? Absolutely. Did Peter belong to Christ. Yes.

The passage in Hebrews 6 is not about God's refusal to accept somebody who has repented. It is about somebody who has willfully walked away from God and refuses to repent. The Bible constantly tells us that salvation is a free gift, that it's not by works but by faith that we are saved. Yet, the Bible also constantly tells us to obey God and listen to Him and seek Him. God works in us - and we work out our salvation with fear and trembling:

> *Wherefore, my beloved, as ye have always obeyed, not as in my presence only, but now much more in my absence, work out your own salvation with fear and trembling. For it is God which worketh in you both to will and to do of his good pleasure.*
>
> Philippians 2:12-13

The Price of Salvation:

Should we ever have to fear that God is going to throw us away? No, precious believer. We should never fear that. God gave His Son for us because He loves us and He wants us to be saved. He didn't pay some little, piddly price for us. The price for our salvation was His only Son.

We matter to God more than we can ever imagine. Do you realize that? We matter to God, and He does not want to lose us. God is not willing that anybody should perish. He wants us to be saved more than we want to be saved. He wants us to be with Him. The problem is not God's love for us. The problem is our willingness to trust in His love and to give our lives completely into His hands.

What if we sin? Then we ask for forgiveness. We run to Christ immediately and seek forgiveness and cleansing and healing. Proverbs 24:16 says, *"For a just man falleth seven times, and riseth up again:"* The writer of Hebrews knew the incredible grace of God. He urged us:

> *For we have not an high priest which cannot be touched with the feeling of our infirmities; but was in all points tempted like as we are, yet without sin. Let us therefore come boldly unto the throne of grace, that we may obtain mercy, and find grace to help in time of need.*
>
> Hebrews 4:15-16

Things God Doesn't Know

Earlier, I mentioned the things that God can't do. I'm going to be an agitator again, and this time I'm going to describe the things God doesn't know. God knows everything, right? He's omniscient. He knows the words we're going to say before we say them.[37] He knows the end from the beginning.[38] However, there are at least four things God doesn't know:

First, God doesn't know a sin He doesn't hate. God hates sin. Sin is whatever He says it is, by the way, regardless of our favorite social mores of the day. Whether it's homosexuality that is acceptable in one culture, or it's murder and cannibalism that is acceptable in another, God is the one who dictates what is and is not sinful.

Second, God doesn't know a sinner He doesn't love. God may hate cannibalism and brutal murder in Papua New Guinea, but He loves the cannibals. God may hate homosexual acts, but He loves the person with same-sex attraction. He loves you and me no matter what we have done and no matter what cruel and dishonest and immoral things we have in our background. He loves us. He wants to save our lives and cleanse us and hold us to His heart.

Third, God doesn't know a path to His throne but through His Son. If there was any other path, then Jesus' prayer in the Garden of Gethsemane wasn't answered. Jesus pleaded, sweating blood with stress, that if there were any other way so that the events of the coming day could pass from Him, then let it be done.[39] Jesus was in agony over the job that was before Him, and if there was any other way, He wanted God to find it. However, there wasn't any other way, and He submitted to God's will in the matter.

Fourth, there is no better time to commit our lives to Him than right now. Our connection with eternity is not in the future. Our connection with eternity is right now. The past is a memory, the future's a hope. Each of us must hand ourselves over to God. He has us sealed until the day of redemption, but we get the immense relief of handing our sovereignty into His hands every day.

I want God's will done in my life. I want Him to do the work He would love to do. I have complete confidence that God's ideas, God's plans and purposes are so much better than anything

I could ever hope for. I just want to get on board with where He's going.

Chapter 10
A Couple of Pitfalls

Then said Jesus to those Jews which believed on him, If ye continue in my word, then are ye my disciples indeed; And ye shall know the truth, and the truth shall make you free.

John 8:31-32

A complete, well-developed understanding of God's Word is always important. Seemingly small misunderstandings and errors can cause a surprising amount of damage - not just in our own lives, but in the lives of those we touch.

Pitfall 1: Works vs. Righteousness

In many churches, there's an emphasis to repent and rededicate one's life, as though congregants have to regain the salvation which they have lost in the course of daily life. People in this position typically have no assurance of their salvation. They get "saved" every week, because they have no rest in Christ. They have no spiritual peace, and right away that should be a signal that something's wrong, because those things were promised to us.

> *Peace I leave with you, my peace I give unto you: not as the world giveth, give I unto you. Let not your heart be troubled, neither let it be afraid.*
>
> John 14:27

On the other hand, it's a veritable plague when we find Christians who have convinced themselves they've reached a state of sinless perfection. This is contrary to 1 John 1:

> *If we say that we have no sin, we deceive ourselves, and the truth is not in us. If we confess our sins, he is faithful and just to forgive us our sins, and to cleanse us from all unrighteousness.*
>
> 1 John 1:8-9

We cannot allow a sense of spiritual superiority to infect us, misdirecting us from our calling as Christians. We are to be the light of the world, filled with the mercy of God through the Holy Spirit. We should be ministering to a broken and suffering world, serving as God's hands to people who need to know His kindness and forgiveness and life-saving power. We cannot do that job - and we actually cause serious damage - if we're wrapped up in our own pride. There is no place for self-righteousness in the kingdom of God.

A works-equals-righteousness kind of theology leads to fear and insecurity, or pride and haughtiness. These are not the fruits we should produce as God's children. Many believers live in needless fear, because they wonder time and again whether they are truly saved. These imagine that God is rubbing a hole through their names in the Book of Life after repeatedly erasing and rewriting it. Each time they sin, every time they discover anything un-Christlike in themselves, anytime they feel emotionally separated from God, they worry they have lost their salvation.

We need to understand how vastly God values us. When we turn away from Him, He longs for us as a father longs for His children. He wants us with Him always, and He wants nothing more than for us to come home to Him. We don't understand that, like the prodigal son, He rejoices to run to us and throw His arms around us. He has a robe and a fatted calf just waiting for us.

The fact is that you and I can know for certain that we are God's children. We can have confidence that our sins have been forgiven, and our destiny is an eternity in Heaven with Him. The Lord does not want us to doubt His love. He doesn't want us to trust in our own efforts. We absolutely cannot earn our own salvation, and if we cannot earn it, we cannot maintain it.

Can we grieve the Father? Yes. Can we destroy opportunities for rewards? Yes. However, our sins were paid 100% by Jesus Christ on the cross. His last words "It is finished," tell us that our debts were paid in full.

Pitfall 2: Negligence

The focus on election, on the other hand, has lead Calvinists to ignore or even oppose evangelism. What's the use? If we're foreordained for salvation, then why go through the trouble of harvest crusades? If God chooses who is saved and who is not, then why send young people as missionaries to lands afflicted by tsetse flies and malaria? The determinism that's implied by an overemphasis of election can lead to hyper-Calvinists fighting against evangelistic crusades and missions.

A deterministic view of the world leads to strife, division, and argumentation. There are more efforts addressed to calming tensions than loving and caring for a hurting world. The overemphasis of God's sovereignty, at the expense of man's responsibility, portrays a God who is willing to capriciously torture the unsuspecting.

The river of life flows between two banks of extremes. The whole dilemma of this controversy of fate versus free will is that it fails to focus on God's objective. His objective is to have a people that love and trust Him.

The answer is balance - but not just balance. The answer is seeking the heart of God. It's hungering and thirsting for Him, trusting in His love and His purposes. It's recognizing that God's will is greater than anything we could ever imagine, and handing Him our sovereignty. It's saying every day, "Father, my life belongs to You.

Lead me today. Show me how to be Your hands to my family and friends. Show me how to reach out to this lost and dying world."

The Seven Letters

We can do a study of the errors in church history. As we look into the past, we discover each error is built on a lack of balance.

I'm fascinated with the seven letters of seven churches in the book of Revelation 2-3. Jesus Christ dictated to John a set of seven report cards for churches in Asia Minor, and I believe all seven churches were surprised by what they heard. Some thought they were doing worse than they were, while some thought they were doing better. Two of the churches had only good said about them. Two of the churches had nothing good said about them. Three had both good things and things they needed to work on. All were churches who claimed the name of Jesus Christ, yet five of them had problems they needed to address.

These seven letters were written to actual churches in first century. These were real churches with real problems. Each letter has the phrase, "He that hath an ear, let him hear what the Spirit says to the churches," however, which tells us they were meant to admonish the churches to whom they were addressed, but also were meant to be heard by all the churches. The letters seem to have an additional level: representing the church age and the problems we find in different church periods throughout the past 2000 years. The seven letters write out church history in advance, which I find fascinating.

These letters also speak to all of us individually. We can see ourselves in these churches, and the warnings and promises Jesus Christ gives them are the same warnings and promises He could give us. The church of Ephesus was patient, hard-working, and dedicated to the truth. Jesus had one thing against them - they had laid aside the love with which they had started following Christ. Jesus tells them to get that love back. We can all take heed to those words. In all our work of "doing church" we cannot forget that loving our God, loving our Savior, loving the people for whom Christ died - that's the center of it all.

These seven letters are valuable to study.[40] Read Revelation 2-3 and carefully examine the things Jesus said to each church. Pay attention to the titles Jesus gives Himself in each letter, His words of praise and admonition, His warnings and promises. I encourage you to read up on the history of each of these churches and their particular struggles.

This is one of the reasons, by the way, I don't take the writings of the early church leaders necessarily as inspired truth. I trust the writings of the apostles, sent by Christ Himself to spread the Gospel to the world. However, we can see by the time John wrote Revelation in A.D. 96 that most of the churches were already off the mark. The early church fathers offer some interesting reading, and their writings give us historical insight. However, we shouldn't build doctrines from them. We build our doctrines from the Word of God.

Chapter 11
The Prodigal Son

I'd like to look at a familiar parable that Jesus tells in Luke 15, one that has some ramifications that many people miss. We all know about the Prodigal Son. What is a prodigal? It's somebody who spends recklessly, as the younger son does in this story:

> *And he said, A certain man had two sons: And the younger of them said to his father, Father, give me the portion of goods that falleth to me. And he divided unto them his living. And not many days after the younger son gathered all together, and took his journey into a far country, and there wasted his substance with riotous living.*
>
> Luke 15:11-13

First of all, it was an audacious, disrespectful thing for the younger son to seek his inheritance while his father was still alive. The father gives in, but it was still quite vulgar in that culture. What does the young man do with his father's money? He throws big parties, buys himself a Lamborghini. He pretends he's a rock star - until the money runs out.

> *And when he had spent all, there arose a mighty famine in that land; and he began to be in want. And he went and joined himself to a citizen of that country; and he sent him into his fields to feed swine. And he would fain have filled his belly with the husks that the swine did eat: and no man gave unto him.*

> Luke 15:14-16

As soon as his funds are tapped out, the young man's friends magically disappear. Nobody takes him in, and he's forced to go make himself a servant. Not only does he have to go feed the animals, but the animals are pigs. He's still Jewish, and he is now having to feed unclean swine out in the fields. He's so hungry he would eat the pig food, but he doesn't even get that much. We Gentiles have to be careful not to miss things because we fail to see things from a Jewish perspective. In the Gentile mind, this is pretty bad, but in the Jewish mind it's as desperately low as anybody can get.

At this point, the young man's ego is absolutely gone, and he finally comes to his senses:

> *And when he came to himself, he said, How many hired servants of my father's have bread enough and to spare, and I perish with hunger! I will arise and go to my father, and will say unto him, Father, I have sinned against Heaven, and before thee, And am no more worthy to be called*

*thy son: make me as one of thy hired
servants.*

Luke 15:17-19

He has an epiphany. His father's servants are treated well, and he might as well go seek to be hired in his father's house. He's truly humbled at this point, and he also feels that he's lost his sonship. He's no longer worried about what he'll look like. He just knows he'll be better off if he can just get hired as a servant. He plans out what he's going to say, and he makes the trip home.

And he arose, and came to his father. But when he was yet a great way off, his father saw him, and had compassion, and ran, and fell on his neck, and kissed him.

Luke 15:20

The young man is ready to give his speech, but the father doesn't even let him get it out. He runs and grabs him, hugging him and kissing him. The son is full of shame over his foolishness and failure. He recognizes how badly he's behaved, but the father doesn't care about all that. He's just glad to have his son home again.

*And the son said unto him, Father, I have
sinned against Heaven, and in thy sight,
and am no more worthy to be called thy
son. But the father said to his servants,
Bring forth the best robe, and put it
on him; and put a ring on his hand,*

> *and shoes on his feet: And bring hither the
> fatted calf, and kill it; and let us eat,
> and be merry: For this my son was dead,
> and is alive again; he was lost, and is
> found. And they began to be merry.*
>
> Luke 15:21-24

There are a few different dimensions here. No matter how badly the young man had fallen, he didn't lose his sonship. Satan tries to convince us that our sin is too big for God to love us. He works hard to keep us from going back to our Father, reminding us of our sin over and over. The best thing we can do is ignore those whispers, and humbly go fall at God's feet.

> *Be afflicted, and mourn, and weep:
> let your laughter be turned to mourning,
> and your joy to heaviness. Humble
> yourselves in the sight of the Lord,
> and he shall lift you up.*
>
> James 4:9-10

New Christians suffer from a typical trap. When they first repent and sincerely ask God to forgive their sins through Christ, they are filled with joy and peace. Then, a few days or weeks or months go by, and something catastrophic happens. They screw up and do something rotten and shameful. That's when Satan has a field day, because new Christians can easily feel that they're all cleaned up and taken care of up until that point. Then they realize they still have problems. They've stumbled and sinned, and they're confronted with their own continued frailty. They believe they're in huge trouble now. We've all been there. We've all felt like we've sinned in a way that's too terrible to be forgiven, and we want to hide from God.

I'm indebted to Hal Lindsey for a particularly precious insight. When shame hits us, we need to ask ourselves this question, "How many of my sins were yet future when Jesus hung on the cross?" The answer is, "All of them." He died for all of them.

When we come to Jesus Christ and receive Him as our Savior, our sins are forgiven, including the ones we commit next Tuesday. That's not a license to sin, of course. "God forbid!" Paul says in Romans 6. However, when we fall, we know we can go right to our Father who loves us, seek His forgiveness and continue walking hand in hand with Him.

Chapter 12
Triangles and Time

When we deal with the paradox between God's destiny for us and our own free will, I find that physics offers us some help. When we understand a little more about the nature of our universe, we can see where God's sovereignty and man's sovereignty can easily coincide.

How many degrees are there in a triangle? Our high school geometry teachers taught us that the corners of a triangle always add up to 180°. If we know the angles of two corners, we can easily figure out the angle of the third corner. That's basic Euclidean geometry.

Trigonometry

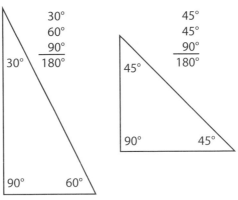

What if we get a transit, go out into a large field, and lay out a large triangle? We very carefully measure it and bring back the three angles. When we add them up, we expect them to add up to 180°, but find instead that those three angles add up to 200°. We recheck our measurements, and our angles still add up to 200°. Why? The laws of mathematics don't change. No, we have simply run into the curvature of the earth. We look at our field and assume that it is flat, but we are no longer dealing with flat, plane geometry. We are dealing with three-dimensions, and triangles in three dimensions can add up to more than 180°.

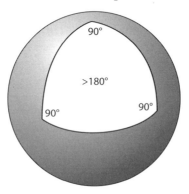

Euclidean geometry is useful, but we do not actually live in a world of only two dimensions. In fact, we don't live in a world of only three dimensions. Dr. Einstein gave us the mathematical insight to be able to describe the world in four dimensions by adding time to the mix. Physicists no longer speak of space and time, but of the fabric of space-time. Time is a physical property.

Einstein went to his grave frustrated by some other problems, which would have been unraveled for him if he had added an additional dimension and moved on to five dimensions. The Kaluza-Kline theory of gravitation and electromagnetism uses five dimensions to explain our universe. The physicists were thus able to unify gravitation and electromagnetism mathematically and create a more elegant model of the universe. There may be as many as 11 dimensions, if not more.

We make the mistake of looking at the universe from the perspective of four-dimensional beings. We think of time as linear and absolute. We can see the spatial dimensions of length, width, and height are bi-directional. We can go both up and down, right and left, back and forth. Time is a strange dimension, because we can only move forward and look back. How many of us can remember tomorrow?

We assume that time is linear and it doesn't change. We assume that an hour a thousand years ago is the same as an hour a thousand years from now. We take time for granted. When we were in school, our teachers showed us timelines. We drew a line on the blackboard from left to right. The left end was the beginning of something, the birth of a person or the founding of a nation. The right end of that line was the death of that person or the termination of that empire.

Because of that experience, we think of time as a line that starts at infinity on the left and proceeds to infinity on the right. When we think of God, we think of somebody who has lots of time. We think of eternity as "a lot of time." That turns out to be bad physics.

A Little Relativity

Did you know that if I raise an atomic clock into the air by one meter, it speeds up by one part in 10^{16}? Time is a physical property. It's affected by gravity. If I raise it up 100 meters, it speeds up by one part in 10^{14}. We shouldn't adjust our calendars over these amounts, but time changes predictably, because it is affected by mass, acceleration, and gravity.

This is not just theoretical stuff. Engineers have to take relativity into consideration when they design telecommunications systems. Satellites are zooming around the planet Earth at tremendous speeds. The differences in time for the satellites in orbit and communication systems on the ground must be calculated or signals are missed. It is the accuracy of the cesium atomic clocks tied to satellites that allows the precision of our GPS devices. You can thank Einstein for our cell phones.

Wait for a moment, though. Is God affected by mass or acceleration or gravity? No. God is not subject to these forces. He is outside them, because He lives in more than our four dimensions. He has much greater dimensionality, and He exists outside the domain of space-time itself.

God is not somebody with a lot of time. He is somebody untouched by time. He is outside of time. That's what Isaiah means when he says in Isaiah 57:15 that God "inhabiteth eternity." That's why the Lord is able to say, *"I am Alpha and Omega, the beginning and the end."*[41]

If God has the technology to create us in the first place, He has the technology to get a message to us. He has given us 66 books penned by 40 different guys over thousands of years that we now discover is an integrated message system. Every number, every place name, every detail, even the implied punctuation we now discover is there by a supernatural engineering.

More important than that, the Bible has its origin from outside time altogether. We know this because God sees the end from the beginning, and He tells us things millennia before they come to pass. We cannot use the Bible as a divination device, or to set dates. However, we can use prophecy to authenticate the entire message. God was able to authenticate His Word by writing history before it happens in the form of predictive prophecy.

When we look at the apparent contradiction between Calvinism and Arminianism, or between predestination and free choice, we find that the paradox goes away when we are able to get past our own four-dimensional thinking. We look at things from inside the domain of space-time, and we do not fully appreciate that God can see past all our limitations. He knows in advance all the decisions that we are going to make, and He leaves us free to make those decisions.

One fellow who has little excuse to be confused by this was John Calvin himself. John Calvin said:

"Therefore we again state that the Word, conceived beyond the beginning of time by God, has perpetually resided with him. By this, his eternity, his true essence, and his divinity are proved."[42]

John Calvin recognized that time is finite and God is eternal. He recognized that God is everlasting and that time itself is a created thing with a beginning. I think that's kind of interesting.

Chapter 13
The Door to Heaven

A man by the name of H. A. Ironside summarized the paradox about fate versus free will graphically without the benefit of modern physics. He described our opportunity for salvation as a door. He said it's as if he's walking down a hall, and he comes to a door in the wall. Over the door it says, "Whosoever will may enter." He looks at that door, and he can either go in or not go in. It's his choice. He makes a decision, and he opens the door and walks through.

On the other side, he finds a banquet hall with a feast sumptuously laid out. He walks around the tables, and he finds name cards at every place setting. After looking over the names, he is startled to find a place setting with his own name on the card. He's astounded to learn that he's expected. How did they know he was coming? He could have chosen not to open the door. Then, he turns and looks at the door he just came through. On the other side, remember, it had said, "Whosoever will may enter." However, he sees that on this side it's labeled, "Foreordained before the foundation of the world."

This is not The Twilight Zone. This is the paradox that is explained because God knows the end from the beginning. We have choices to make, but God already knows what those choices will be. He's known from the beginning who are His - the ones who will be with Him in eternity. From our side of the door, we have a chance to open the door or not. From His side of the door, we were foreordained from the beginning of time.

Human Software

Imagine a personal computer. Imagine we know everything there is to know about every circuit, every wire, every part of that hardware. Would that tell us anything about its behavior? Absolutely not, because the hardware is simply a residence for something else called software. The software determines which programs the computer runs. The hardware is the engine that gives the software the ability to run the programs it needs to run.

We can put software on CDs or on thumb drives. These days we download software over the Internet. Suppose I had a blank thumb drive and a sensitive postal scale. Let's say I put that thumb drive on the postal scale, and it weighs exactly one ounce. Then, let's say I load that software with 10 GB worth of digital pictures and videos. When I put the thumb drive back on the postal scale, it will still weigh exactly one ounce. Why? Software has no mass. Its embodiment at some instant may reflect mass, but it has no mass. I can sit in a coffee shop and use their WiFi, and I can send information through the air. It travels up into space, hits satellites, and bounces back.

If I look at a crowd of people, I cannot see the software, the true essence of those people. I can see the temporary residences they are dwelling in, but I can't see the real them. The real us is software, not hardware. This shell we're living in is a temporary hard drive.

I had an interesting experience a few years ago. I had a rigorous schedule back then, and I did a lot of writing. I was very dependent on my laptop, because it allowed me to do writing while I traveled. After a few years of hard use, my laptop finally died. I took it to the shop to get fixed, but it had booted up for the last time. I was in trouble, because I depended on my laptop and I couldn't afford a new one. Some friends of the ministry sensed that I was in trouble, and they graciously offered me a new flash-and-dash laptop with all the bells and whistles. I was more grateful for this than I can tell you.

I'll never forget the day that I unpacked it and fired it up. I started loading it with all the software that I had collected - 20 years of tools - and I was back in business on familiar terms. All the files I was used to were there for me, except that they ran about a hundred times faster.

That experience left an impression on me, and it hit me with a realization: we are all heading for an upgrade. Software has no mass. The real us has no mass. This means that software is not affected by time. One day we are going to junk our old hardware, but the part of us that is eternal will be transferred.

You and I are eternal, whether we like it or not. That's good news for those who are saved, but it's terrible news if we're not. As human beings we face the prospect of two deaths, not just one. We are all familiar with the first death, but that's not the death that should concern us. The second death is the one that is terrifying.

Resurrection

We all know about DNA, the code for life. When an egg is fertilized, it becomes a zygote and goes through mitosis, splitting and growing, splitting and growing. The two cells become four, and the four cells become eight. After a little while something fascinating happens. The cells begin to differentiate into different body parts. Pretty soon we see the line that will become the backbone grow down the middle. Some cells become bone tissue and some become heart muscle. Each new cell starts taking its role necessary for an entire body to develop. This is staggering considering the fact that the exact same DNA reproduces in each cell during mitosis. Identical strands of DNA are created over and over again, yet certain sections are expressed in one set of cells while other sections are expressed in other sets as the body forms the lungs and kidneys and eyes. It's all pre-programmed, and it's quite amazing.

Most westerners have seen the Jurassic Park movies, where DNA from dinosaurs has been turned into full dinosaurs. God has the technology to do that, if He wanted. He could resurrect our bodies with just a little bit of DNA. However, even if He had a full body that looked like me, there would be something missing. The hardware of our bodies is brilliantly put together, but our hardware is nothing without our software. Even if your bodies were resurrected because somebody cloned our DNA, that new body wouldn't be you.

Salvation

We are going to spend eternity either in the presence of God or out of the presence of God. How do we make sure we're going to be ushered into the presence of God when we cast off this mortal coil? No problem. We just have to be perfect.

Walter Martin used to irreverently say that there are two ways to get to Heaven, Plan A and Plan B:

Plan A is: "You never screw up from the time of your accountability onwards. You never make a mistake." Whether we're tired or stressed out, whether people are unkind to us and treat us unjustly, we simply go through all the contingencies of life without ever doing anything wrong. If we are successful, then we can march right through the pearly gates of Heaven, walk up to God and say, "Hello. Please move over. Now there's two of us."

Plan B is: "Accept your pre-paid ticket." In Plan B, we embrace God's willingness to impute the righteousness of Jesus Christ to us.

Which one is actually possible? This was Walter's way of making his point. Unless we live in a world of self-delusion, we recognize that Plan A is exceptionally improbable, and only one man has ever done it. The rest of us don't get through life without errors. John and Paul both said it well for us:

> *If we say that we have no sin, we deceive ourselves, and the truth is not in us.*
>
> 1 John 1:8

> *For all have sinned, and come short of the glory of God;*
>
> Romans 3:23

Those who have accepted the redemption that God has provided are in for some real excitement. It's going to be tremendous fun, because we're going to be joint heirs with Him. We have no ability to grasp the joy that will be involved in joining with Christ in the eternal work He's doing.

Those who are not in Jesus Christ have a big, big problem, because they are subject to a genetic defect. The major problem today isn't being born

HIV-positive. Our biggest problem is that we're born sin-positive. We have a genetic defect from our father Adam, and the only cure is the blood of Jesus Christ. When we receive Jesus Christ as our Lord and Savior, putting away our pride and seeking his forgiveness, we're accepted into eternity. Faith isn't just recognizing our sin; it's understanding that God wants to forgive us and rejoices to bring us into His fold.

Each one of us can be assured of our salvation without even leaving our seats. In the privacy of our own will, we can commit ourselves into the hands of the Father who will seal our eternities.

The differences between Arminianism and Calvinism on eternal security are academic. Why do I say that? If someone apparently becomes a Christian, apparently shows some fruit, and then falls away, the Calvinist will say that that person wasn't truly born again in the first place. The Arminian says that the person was either not born again or turned away from God and has lost his salvation. However, nobody knows the true situation except for God Himself. Only He knows the goings on in the heart, and only He knows those who were always His.

Chapter 14

The Fruit We Bear

We are not always excited about our own sovereignty. There is a great deal of responsibility involved in this gift that God has given us. What are we supposed to do with it? The best thing we can do, the wisest and most beneficial thing we can do is to give it right back to God. We can say, "Lord, thank You. Here is my life. Take it. I want to be Yours. You alone know the end from the beginning. You alone know what's best for me."

Chuck Smith used to tell a story about a school reunion he went to. When he was in school, he had a big crush on a girl there. He used to pray that if God would help get this girl to like him, he would do anything. It was the usual teenage prayer: "Boy, Lord. If You'll do this thing for me..." Apparently the girl had her own ideas, and it didn't work out the way Chuck prayed. Many years later, he attended a reunion where he met up with that woman he'd had a crush on, and he realized she would not have been right for him. He was courteous as he spoke to her, but in his privacy he went to the Lord and said, "Thank You, Lord, for the prayers You don't answer."

We all have prayers that God didn't answer the way we wanted, and we don't know why. I suspect that list is substantial for many of us. Sometimes we've lost loved ones. Sometimes we've lost jobs and houses and cars. There are prayers that the Lord in His wisdom chooses not to answer our way, and sometimes that has frustrated us or broken our hearts.

We are sovereign. We have our own wills, our desires, our ideas. We have the things we would do if we were in charge. However, the God of the Bible sees the end from the beginning, and we're wise to put our lives completely in His hands and to say, as Jesus said in the Garden of Gethsemane, *"Nevertheless, not as I will, but as Thou wilt."*[43]

Jesus also calls us to be His disciples, to take up our crosses daily to follow Him - and to count the cost before we do so.

> *And whosoever doth not bear his cross,*
> *and come after me, cannot be my disciple.*
> *For which of you, intending to build a*
> *tower, sitteth not down first, and counteth*
> *the cost, whether he have sufficient to*
> *finish it?*
>
> Luke 14:27-28

This is a sobering verse, because it reminds us that to be Christ's disciples we need to be willing to suffer if He asks us to. We must be willing to set aside our pride, our desires, our will to follow Him. Jesus also tells us in Matthew 11:29-30 to pick up His yoke, the yoke He gives us. There is immediate comfort because He also says that His yoke is easy and His burden is light. Yet, there is definitely a sense of personal responsibility here - in choosing to carry our cross - and in choosing to carry the light burdens Christ gives to us.

Living for Christ day by day can be difficult, and yet it is the greatest adventure in the world. We are in a brutal spiritual battle, but Jesus has already given us the victory. The sweat and tears are worth it. When Jesus died on that cross, it saved the entire world. When we submit to His purposes in our lives, He does amazing things in us - things we could never have even hoped for.

Bearing Fruit

We are in a dangerous place when we try to decide who is saved and who isn't. God knows everyone who repents and follows Him in the end. However, there is something we can do. We can inspect people's fruit. We're not even supposed to inspect the gifts of the Spirit. We're supposed to inspect the fruits of the Spirit.

> *But the fruit of the Spirit is love, joy, peace, longsuffering, gentleness, goodness, faith, Meekness, temperance: against such there is no law. And they that are Christ's have crucified the flesh with the affections and lusts. If we live in the Spirit, let us also walk in the Spirit.*
>
> Galatians 5:22-25

Am I really committed to the Lord Jesus Christ? Have I honestly handed Him the Lordship of my life? Am I abiding in Christ? Is there fruit of that in my life? It's good to do a self-check now and then. What about you? If you're not sure, then make Him the priority of your life right now. Ask Him to pay for your sins and fill you with His Holy Spirit. We know God gives the Holy Spirit to those who ask because He loves to give us the good things we need.[44]

Once we've done that, then what? We remember that Jesus Christ is our first love. We thank Him every day for His love, for His mercy, for His power to work in our lives to do His will. We trust in Him, and we give Him our lives every day. "Here, Lord. Here is my life. Do with it today what You will."

I really believe that you and I can leave this room with the assurance of salvation. We do not have to fear that God will toss us away. However, we also have assurance because we give the whole-hearted, comprehensive commitment of our sovereignty into the hands of Jesus Christ. Each one of us needs to do that, and we need to do it every day.

When we do, guess what? He produces fruit in us. He points out the people in our lives that need our help. He helps us know when to say "No" to this person or group so we can focus over here on this person or group. He works in us patience, kindness, gentleness, and love. When we are planted by the streams of water that are His Spirit, we will bear beautiful fruit.

The problem isn't that Christians don't know what good fruit looks like. We just forget that God is the one who produces it in us. Too often, westop focusing on Him and start focusing on the works themselves, and that's where we get into trouble. When we try to produce fruit without Him, depending on our own righteousness, we find that we produce nasty fruit that nobody wants to eat. We become harsh, self-righteous, and judgmental. We become hypocrites, falling into the very sins we've condemned others for doing.[45] We can do church every week and say all the right things, but nobody wants to hear what we have to say because there is no love in our lives.[46] It's only by walking hand in hand with Christ every day that we can grow to produce the sweet fruit of His Spirit.[47]

We find in Matthew 25 a parable that brings this difference to light. The parable describes a future day when Jesus divides the sheep from the goats. Both the sheep and the goats call Jesus, "Lord," but only the sheep are given the kingdom, which Jesus declares was prepared "from the foundation of the world." The difference between the sheep and the goats is quite simple. The sheep bore the fruit of God's love:

> *When the Son of man shall come in his glory, and all the holy angels with him, then shall he sit upon the throne of his*

> *glory: And before him shall be gathered all nations: and he shall separate them one from another, as a shepherd divideth his sheep from the goats: And he shall set the sheep on his right hand, but the goats on the left. Then shall the King say unto them on his right hand, Come, ye blessed of my Father, inherit the kingdom prepared for you from the foundation of the world: For I was an hungred, and ye gave me meat: I was thirsty, and ye gave me drink: I was a stranger, and ye took me in: Naked, and ye clothed me: I was sick, and ye visited me: I was in prison, and ye came unto me. Then shall the righteous answer him, saying, Lord, when saw we thee an hungred, and fed thee? or thirsty, and gave thee drink? When saw we thee a stranger, and took thee in? or naked, and clothed thee? Or when saw we thee sick, or in prison, and came unto thee? And the King shall answer and say unto them, Verily I say unto you, Inasmuch as ye have done it unto one of the least of these my brethren, ye have done it unto me.*
>
> Matthew 25:31-40

The goats also call Jesus, "Lord." However, the goats did not bear the fruit of God's love. They didn't have compassion or concern for others. We can surmise that the goats were too focused on themselves to care about the needs of others.

They were talking the talk, but they were not walking with Christ. We can't walk with Christ without getting infected by the love and concern He has for people.[48]

> *Then shall he say also unto them on the left hand, Depart from me, ye cursed, into everlasting fire, prepared for the devil and his angels: For I was an hungred, and ye gave me no meat: I was thirsty, and ye gave me no drink: I was a stranger, and ye took me not in: naked, and ye clothed me not: sick, and in prison, and ye visited me not. Then shall they also answer him, saying, Lord, when saw we thee an hungred, or athirst, or a stranger, or naked, or sick, or in prison, and did not minister unto thee? Then shall he answer them, saying, Verily I say unto you, Inasmuch as ye did it not to one of the least of these, ye did it not to me. And these shall go away into everlasting punishment: but the righteous into life eternal.*
>
> Matthew 25:41-46

Our righteousness can never save us, because we have a sin defect. Only the covenant made by Christ's blood can save us. However, those who are born again, who are "planted by the streams of water," fed by the Holy Spirit - they will be like the tree in Psalm 1 that bears its fruit in season and whose leaf never withers. When we are born again, fully committed to loving our Savior, He will produce fruit naturally through us. As we walk with Christ day by day, the Holy Spirit will do the work of slowly pruning off those unfruitful branches in our hearts. He'll start removing the broken, dead twigs. He will make us people who are truly a blessing to others.

Does that mean we'll never sin again? It's unlikely. We all have turned our eyes away from Jesus Christ at times, and like Peter walking toward Jesus on the water, we've looked at the "wind and the waves" and started to sink.[49] However, Jesus is always right there to catch us when we're floundering and to help us walk safely back to the boat. Our Shepherd has no interest in letting us drown, no matter how bad we feel about ourselves. We simply need to cry out as Peter did, "Lord, save me!" Hopefully, though, our fruit tastes better every year that goes by as we get better at submitting to the Holy Spirit. We can have confidence that while we're abiding in Christ, we're absolutely secure. We're absolutely secure.

The trick is not to focus on the wind and the waves, or even our own particular struggles with sin. The trick is to focus on Christ and trust Him and His patient, constant love for us. When we keep our eyes on Jesus, we not only walk on water, we find we start desiring the things He desires for us.

A Prayer

Father, we praise You for who You are, and we stand in awe of Your handiwork, of Your Word that You've revealed to us. We are grateful for the extremes that You've gone to, that we might live, that we might have fellowship with You, that we might spend an eternity in Your presence. We thank You for that, Father. We also tremble at the gift of sovereignty that You've given us, of our ability to make our own choices. We quickly realize through the ministry of Your Holy Spirit that our capacity for decision-making far exceeds our ability to really comprehend their implications. As we look at ourselves, Father, we realize that we have the genetic defect of sin inherited from our forefather Adam.

Father, we are sinful beings by nature, and whatever efforts we make to earn salvation fall overwhelmingly short. Yet, You have a destiny for us, one that You have provided for us by Your Son, Jesus Christ Himself. We come before Your throne now, Father, and we ask You to receive us by the righteousness imputed to us through Christ. May His blood cover us and wash away our sins. May His blood break the hold of sin on our lives and make us truly free. Be our Father, our

Shepherd, our Guide throughout our entire Life. Seal us by Your Holy Spirit, and make our paths straight. Father, we thank You for opening eternity to us, that we might be with You forever. We commit ourselves afresh into Your hands in the Name of Jesus, our Lord and Savior, amen.

Endnotes

1 - Genesis 2:7, 21-23
2 - Matthew 6:10; Luke 11:2
3 - Jeremiah 33:20-21; Genesis 8:22
4 - 1 Corinthians 14:32
5 - Psalm 138:2
6 - CNN. (1995, November 7). Rabin's Alleged Killer Appears in Court. Retrieved June 01, 2017, from http://www.cnn.com/WORLD/9511/rabin/amir/11-06/
7 - See *Cosmic Codes*, by Chuck Missler.
8 - We cover these codes in more depth in our books *Cosmic Codes*, *Beyond Coincidence*, and *Hidden Treasures*.
9 - Exodus 20:7
10 - Hebrews 11:17-19
11 - Jehovahjireh has also been translated by some as "God will provide," but there is strong support for "Jehovah sees." Strong's H3070 defines it as "Jehovah will see (to it)". Brown-Driver-Brigg's Hebrew Definitions offers only "Jehovah sees." Keil & Delitzsch comment on the verse, writing "The rendering 'on the mount of Jehovah it is provided' is not allowable, for the Niphal of the verb does not mean provideri, but appear. Moreover, in this case the medium of God's seeing or interposition was His appearing." (Keil & Delitzsch. Commentary on the Old Testament (1866). e-Sword commentary. Public Domain.)
12 - Matthew 17:3-5; Mark 9:4-8
13 - Titus 1:2; Hebrews 6:18

14 - Genesis 15:13-18; 26:1-4; 28:10-15

15 - Numbers 14:26-34; Hebrews 3:17-19

16 - 2 Kings 21; 2 Chronicles 33

17 - Matthew 21; Mark 11; Luke 19; John 12

18 - Deuteronomy 16:16

19 - Josephus, F. (A.D. 75). *The Wars of the Jews* (6.9.3).

20 - Isaiah 10:20-22; Joel 2:32; Micah 7:18; Zephaniah 3:13; Zechariah 8:12-13

21 - Genesis 26:4

22 - 1 Kings 19:18; Romans 11:4

23 - Acts 9:1-8; 22:3-10

24 - Exodus 32:31-32; Romans 9:3

25 - Acts 27

26 - Acts 28:30-31

27 - Philippians 4:22

28 - Philemon 1:10

29 - Ruth 1:16

30 - Deuteronomy 23:3

31 - Schaff, P., & Schaff, D. S. (1898). History of the Christian Church: Modern Christianity; the Swiss Reformation (3rd ed., Vol. VII, pp 815-816). New York: Charles Scribern's Sons.

32 - Romans 3:23; 5:12-15

33 - John 1:12-13; Romans 8:14-16

34 - Luke 23:39-43

35 - Titus 3:5

36 - Mark 14:66-72

37 - Psalm 139:4

Endnotes

38 - Isaiah 46:9-10

39 - Matthew 26:38-44; Luke 22:41-44

40 - Our study *The Letters to the Seven Churches* explores Revelation 2-3 in depth.

41 - Revelation 21:6; 22:13

42 - Calvin, J. (1960, 2006). Calvin: Institutes of the Christian Religion (Vol. I, Pg. 131) (J. T. McNeill, Ed.; F. L. Battles, Trans.). Louisville: Westminster John Knox Press.

43 - Matthew 26:39

44 - Luke 11:9-13

45 - 1 Corinthians 10:12; Galatians 6:1

46 - 1 Corinthians 13:1-3

47 - Galatians 5:22-26

48 - 1 John 4:7-8

49 - Matthew 14:25-33

About the Author

Chuck Missler
Founder, Koinonia House

Chuck Missler was raised in Southern California.

Chuck demonstrated an aptitude for technical interests as a youth. He became a ham radio operator at age nine and started piloting airplanes as a teenager. While still in high school, Chuck built a digital computer in the family garage.

His plans to pursue a doctorate in electrical engineering at Stanford University were interrupted when he received a Congressional appointment to the United States Naval Academy at Annapolis. Graduating with honors, Chuck took his commission in the Air Force. After completing flight training, he met and married Nancy (who later founded The King's High Way Ministries). Chuck joined the Missile Program and eventually became Branch Chief of the Department of Guided Missiles.

Chuck made the transition from the military to the private sector when he became a systems engineer with TRW, a large aerospace firm. He then went on to serve as a senior analyst with a non-profit think tank where he conducted projects for the intelligence community and the Department of Defense. During that time, Chuck earned a master's degree in engineering at UCLA, supplementing previous graduate work in applied mathematics, advanced statistics and information sciences.

Recruited into senior management at the Ford Motor Company in Dearborn, Michigan, Chuck established the first international computer network in 1966. He left Ford to start his own company, a computer network firm that was subsequently acquired by Automatic Data Processing (listed on the New York Stock Exchange) to become its Network Services Division.

As Chuck notes, his day of reckoning came in the early '90s when — as the result of a merger — he found himself the chairman and a major shareholder of a small, publicly owned development company known as Phoenix Group International. The firm established an $8 billion joint venture with the Soviet Union to supply personal computers to their 143,000 schools. Due to several unforeseen circumstances, the venture failed. The Misslers lost everything, including their home, automobiles and insurance.

It was during this difficult time that Chuck turned to God and the Bible. As a child he had developed an intense interest in the Bible; studying it became a favorite pastime. In the 1970s, while still in the corporate world, Chuck began leading weekly Bible studies at the 30,000 member Calvary Chapel Costa Mesa, in California. He and Nancy established Koinonia House in 1973, an organization devoted to encouraging people to study the Bible.

Chuck had enjoyed a longtime, personal relationship with Hal Lindsey, who upon hearing of Chuck's professional misfortune, convinced him that he could easily succeed as an independent author and speaker. Over the years, Chuck had developed a loyal following. (Through Doug Wetmore, head of the tape ministry of Firefighters for Christ, Chuck learned that over 7 million copies of his taped Bible studies were scattered throughout the world.) Koinonia House then became Chuck's full-time profession.

Hidden Treasures

For the novice, as well as the sophisticate, this book is full of surprises. It includes subtle discoveries lying just "beneath" the text – hidden messages, encryptions, deliberate misspellings and other amendments to the text – that present implications beyond the immediate context, demonstrating a skillful design that has its origin from outside our space and time. Drawing upon over forty years of collecting, Chuck highlights in this book many of the precious nuggets that have become characteristic of his popular Bible studies around the world.

It is guaranteed to stimulate, provoke, and, hopefully, to disturb. It will confound the skeptic and encourage the believer. It is a "must read" for every thinking seeker of truth and serious inquirer of reality.

Other Resources

Learn the Bible

Are you ready for a detailed yet thoroughly enjoyable study of the most profound book ever written?

Using sound scientific facts, historical analysis, and Biblical narrative, acclaimed teacher Dr. Chuck Missler weaves together a rich tapestry of information—providing an accurate understanding of Scripture's relation to itself, to us and to the world at large.

Examine the heroic tales of Exodus, the lasting wisdom of Proverbs, or even the enigmatic imagery of Revelation with the simple, Scripturally sound insights and fresh perspectives found in *Learn the Bible in 24 Hours*. Whether you want to explore some of the less-discussed nuances of Scripture or you need a comprehensive refresher course on the Bible's themes and stories, *Learn the Bible in 24 Hours* is a great guide.

Available from https://Resources.khouse.org

How We Got Our Bible

- Where did our Bible come from? How good are the texts?
- Why do we believe its origin is supernatural?
- How do we know that it really is the Word of God?
- How accurate are our translations?
- Which version is the best?

Chuck Missler, an internationally recognized Biblical authority, reviews the origin of both the Old and New Testaments in light of recent discoveries and controversies.